The Last Messiah

By C. J. Henning

Other titles by C.J. Henning which can be found

On Amazon.com or Kindle

Common Sense or Who's That Sitting in My Pew

Saga of Everstream

    Tiathan Eiula-War of the Seven Fortresses
        Volumes One and Two

  Whirlwind Sage and the Arbushi Wars

Complete Poetry 1968-2000
Wormwood
On The Morning of the First Day
John Taddlebock and the Weegie Worts
Tittle Tattle Tales
Random Thoughts of an Old Man
Cathedral
Risen and Rising
The Plays by C. J. Henning Vol. One and Two
Fairy Tale and Nursery Rhyme Mysteries

CHAPTER ONE

"Ladies and gentlemen! The President of the United States!" For the first time the top newscaster, Warren P. Long of the National Governmental System for Broadcasting, NGSB, announced the introduction for President Avery. The President himself sat off stage for over an hour revising his speech to the nation.

Inside the gymnasium of Hardwell University sat a few hundred students, reporters and faculty awaiting a new program which they hoped would not affect their positions or take away government scholarships.

President John Avery was a middle aged liberal who believed that the United States would lead the world into a concise financial and political unification whereby peace and the rule of law would bring everyone under the umbrella of one government.

He had thick gray wavy hair, piercing blue eyes, smooth skin with a hint of crow's feet around the eyes and a hint of a bulge around the waist. His wife was always front and center for all to see her support This was the most important speech of his first term in office. He was revered as a national symbol just below the American flag. He waited for the applause to die down before walking to the mass of microphones that stood before him.

"Good evening. Tonight I want to speak to you about the present and ongoing crisis throughout the world." President Avery looked around the room to see who was listening. "We as a nation have enjoyed the many freedoms that our Constitution has afforded us. Now those freedoms are under attack and have divided this country. This country, like it or not, was founded with God in mind, but now we are divided in seeking God's approval or just our own. I am not here to make that decision for it is each of your own belief where you stand. Mine is to protect this country from the enemy within and the enemy without."

A smattering of applause interrupted his speech and he patiently waited for their full attention. President Avery needed to take care how he presented his next executive decision.

"We are in a perilous time whereby terrorist

organizations are trying to destroy the very freedoms we enjoy." Avery looked across the room as cameras clicked and many of the three hundred citizens stared blankly up at him. "We cannot let them destroy us from within. Already we have the bombings in San Francisco, fifteen dead in a church in North Carolina, one hundred and fifty dead in the mall in Minnesota and the firebombing of fifteen churches in Georgia."

The room was full of sighs and clucking of tongues which almost brought a smile to Avery. The next part of his speech was crucial to convincing the country he was on the right path.

"I have signed an executive order whereby every loyal citizen in this country will register their loyalty to local government agencies." Avery saw some mouths open in surprise. "You will be given a choice of a computerized disk, a computer chip implanted in the wrist or your social security number imprinted on your wrist that can only be seen under certain light. There will be a record only you can access unless it involves the security of this nation. A credit score will be established so that we know whether income or work status has been compromised."

Those in attendance started murmuring a bit louder. It appeared this was not going to be easy.

"We already have a data base that has recorded your credit score, education, location and military history." Avery ignored the murmuring and continued. "Some of you are thinking this is not to ensure our freedom, but do not believe them as they may be the very terrorists who wish to undermine this country."

A voice of quiet protest could be heard and a security guard escorted the woman out. Others who sat next to her became silent.

"We cannot be cowered because of the folklore that this may be the mark of the beast." The uneasiness of the audience gave him pause. "I assure you it is not. I consider myself to be of the faith and would never lead you down that path. My advisors tell me that is not where we are heading. Congress has approved my actions. Those that tell you this is a fulfillment of prophesy are wrong. Tell me how else I can protect the American people and I will consider it."

Many of those in front of him became restless and some left the room. Avery sighed audibly into the microphone.

"This is a reality of the times for the security and safety of this nation and I will not ignore or push it aside." Wanting to call back those that left was not an option, but a sign of weakness he refused to show. "I have heard the rumors, but this needed to avoid a world holocaust."

He could hear more discussion among those who stayed. Some started to put on their coats while others looked down at the floor.

"Look people." Avery was becoming impatient. "I don't have horns or a red tail as some conservatives on the right insist. I am just like you and you voted me in this position. I have no reason to lie to you. This country will survive with initiatives we begin with today. Do not be afraid because I offer hope and salvation to our way of life."

No one else left the room. Some shook their heads while others stared blankly. Reporters scribble furiously to make sure they had enough for the evening news.

"Everyone who signs up will be given a tax credit and special privileges in the consumer marketplace." Avery saw the crowd begin to relax. "We cannot let our enemies destroy us from within. If this experiment succeeds the United Nations will expect the world to follow our example. Let us hope that this will bless and honor our forefathers who fought and died so we continue to have the freedom they expected us to have."

No one seemed to be convinced, but it was the TV audience that mattered and the polls tomorrow night. He knew it would not be easy, but it had begun.

"Again, I regret to say that unless we are willing to sacrifice for our country we will never again be free." His voice just an empty echo throughout the hall. "Those who do not follow this option will be considered a possible enemy of the state. Such extremes are necessary. I want to thank you all for the opportunity to speak with you and for your attention. Good night."

The OFF AIR sign lit up as the President Avery wiped his brow and cursed quietly away from the microphone. As Avery's security guards led him away, Patricia Ohlman of PNP took her spot center stage in front of the camera. Ohlman was a twenty-year journalist who could not resist making her own speeches when only a comment would do.

"Good evening, ladies and gentlemen, Patricia Ohlman live at the Civic Center in Minneapolis, Minnesota." She kept a bright smile throughout all her commentaries even if it were bad news. "As you heard the President tonight, we are in a state of crisis, but he failed to elaborate on the real problem. The country has been divided into three factions that deal within the realm of religion, politics and social unrest. Recently there have been protests for the reinstitution of religion in Politics hoping for divine intervention to save America. We have the Patriots for Christ, The Papal See Converts and the Preservation of Jesus in Politics who all want an overhaul of the government."

"Each of these radical group refuse to acknowledge or will adhere to the new executive action." Ohlman kept a more solemn look as she presented her case. "The Foundation of the Son of Man are the only ones led by two men who call themselves Joshua and Abraham that have accepted and promoted the executive action of President Avery. Most of the country has mocked all these groups as being outside the reality of every day citizens. The mood of the country according to the latest Gaines Poll is that few care what the government does and will act accordingly."

"Congress does not have the will to change anything in the executive action and will most likely pass whatever it would take to protect the American people." Ohlman brought back her award winning smile. "This is Patricia Ohlman, PNP News, coming from Hardwell University saying good night."

Ohlman turned and walked away to a vacant hallway leading to the parking lot. The camera crew started pack up and leave while the technicians stayed behind working on soundbites. The main studio shut down the link and lights went on as Joseph Strine, Angela Alcutt and Wendell Shore set up their notes and waited for their cues. Angela Alcutt was the anchor person, a no nonsense blonde with a PHD in history and communications. Her piercing blue eyes mesmerized most of those she interviewed so she could extract more information than any other reporter. It helped that she wore short skirts showing off the greatest legs in the business. No one thought it sexist, just another weapon to find out the truth.

Joseph Strine was a token old fashioned reporter whose 50 years of journalism was now obsolete in the new modern world. His folksy humor was legendary and his encyclopedia memory was necessary in obscure news stories. He still had a full head of gray hair with walrus type mustache, but looked years longer than seventy-two.

Wendell Shore was a forty-two-year old black male

who knew how to break down stories and lean them in any direction he cared to do. President Avery met with him three times in the last year to help clarify his message. Shore could convince almost anyone that an orange was really a lemon in disguise.

"Good evening ladies and gentlemen, we have a number of events to cover tonight." Alcutt stared into the souls of all who had tuned in. "But we have been privy to a tape concerning the open air meeting in Duffy Square by Archbishop John Corbin to a crowd of thousands. Here now is Harold Bunker at the scene."

The tape starts showing a red faced jovial looking man of thirty-two, divorced and living in his office spending his time reading literature from the 1940's and '50's. It seemed a simpler time for the world. He was just a reporter who did not feel the need to hone up on the people he covered and interviewed, but he was the son of the station's vice president.

"Here in Duffy Square," Harold didn't even introduce himself. "in New York City, you are watching an estimated one hundred thousand citizens awaiting the arrival of their new guru, Archbishop John J. Corbin leader of the Foundation of the Son of Man. Archbishop Corbin, you might remember, worked hard for the passage of the Corbin Law. Archbishop Corbin was the first clergyman of the Children to personally lobby for a major bill and succeeded."

Joshua has given Archbishop Corbin the honor of relaying the news to the many followers who gathered here tonight since they are unaware at the moment of the impending news. We, also…. Wait a minute. I think the Archbishop is going to be introduced and…." Bunker had started toward the platform and in so doing pulled the connection to his microphone. The cameramen followed him through the crowd unaware that he was disconnected.

Archbishop John J. Corbin walked up to the podium having a strong presence though a man of forty-two with look of someone twenty years older. A former church minister for fifteen years and then a treasurer for the Foundation of the Son of Man. Corbin had long been overdue to be Archbishop with all the reforms and recognition by the leaders. Looking confidently at his audience and listening to their applause, Corbin smiled hearing "Praise God!" and Praise the Lord!" It was almost as if the praise was for him alone.

"And all the people said?" Corbin raised his arms with eyes blazing with fire.

"Amen!" The crowd shouted enthusiastically.

"Good evening brothers and sisters!" Corbin smugly glanced over the multitude before him. "We are gathered here tonight for a very momentous occasion to the opening of our three-day services here in New York City. The best news possible is the passing of a bill I presented to Congress. Due to the disturbance of violence and rioting in most of the cities here in the United States, Congress has made into law that all patriots and Christians identify themselves with an armband or bracelet or imprints on one's forehead or wrist to show their allegiance to the state."

A faint murmuring from the crowd did not go unnoticed by Corbin who scoured the masses to see if he could identify those who might be a problem. Of course, the many cameras around him would later determine those who might object.

"Enemies who would disrupt our society must be weeded out for the safety of everyone else." Corbin's voice lowered to enhance the seriousness of the situation.

Corbin raised his hands to calm the crowd before

continuing to speak. "The government has asked me to give you more information about these arm bands we are wearing. This is not the sign of the Anti-Christ as some have told you." Corbin tapped the black and gold armband. "Look! It is in the shape of a Cross and a sword! It is the sign of faith and allegiance to those who represent rule this country."

"We have worked out a program to show a need for identification so that those who fight against us would have to come to us for their food, clothing, work…anything that will allow them to hide from us." Corbin heard the murmuring again.

"I hope and pray that those of you who question the legality of this law that you have to realize that this is our God's intervention. We are the one and only true faith." Corbin gave his most sincere smile and condescending stare. "No help will be given and no sanctuary will be offered to anyone who does not wear the armband. For those who tell you this is the mark of the beast, be realistic. If I said you were to be imprinted on the hand and forehead, I would expect you to resist."

"Brothers and sisters," Corbin lifted his arms and waited for everyone to do the same. "Pray with me now for the touch of our God upon his people for we are in troubled and dangerous times. The armbands will be distributed in every town all throughout this country. You can refuse, but I would advise against it. There are traitors all around us."

Many in the crowd nodded agreement and some moved closer to the podium hoping to touch the sacred robe of Archbishop Corbin.

"We, of the Foundation of the Son of Man, have been given this sign," Corbin raised one of the armbands. "to celebrate our Lord and Master to show our devotion and love for the rest of our lives to him who leads us even now. Show all men your faith by wearing this emblem of peace. Praise God!"

Here the crowd reacts and cheers as Corbin expected them to. He smiles and holds up an armband showing only the side of the sword.

"Glory! Glory! Glory!" Many started to chant and reached out for the many armbands, bracelets and even necklaces being passed around. Others cried out to be forgiven for their doubts about Corbin and the state.

Corbin became part of the crowd as sweat poured from his face as he zealously continued to speak.

"As long as this symbol is on our arms or around our necks, you need not fear anyone. All you have to do is obey the new prophets of our God which will be sent to be around you. They will preach your God's will in your lives. Praise God that these men and women still dream dreams and have visions that they themselves can interpret as an act of God so you know we are His children!"

The masses applaud in approval with shouts of "Praise God!" and "Thank you, God!" Many moved forward only to be pushed back by armed guards who not very gentle in protecting Archbishop Corbin.

"Now, let us bring our hearts and minds to pray for our Master…." A shot rang out splintering part of the podium. No one moved until the first group near the front began to run and then muffled confusion as the Archbishop was covered by his security guards.

"How can you speak of God!" a women's voice is heard from a window across the street. "When you don't even know what it means to love? We wouldn't touch that armband….."

A second shot rang out hitting the woman with the rifle who fell to her death from the window. A few men from the crowd below ran into the building. Breaking down the apartment door, a second woman stood with gun in hand. She fired once missing them until they wrestled her to the floor.

Bringing her downstairs, they found out her name was Grace Leah Armstrong who was a twenty-two-year old revolutionary known for firebombing many of the Children's religious sites. As a member of the Patriots of Christ, Grace had been arrested many times for smaller offences and served time with the local police.

Corbin recognized her right away as she was dragged away. He waved his hand to the men, beckoning them to come to his side. Grace was brought through the crowd who insulted and slapped as she passed.

Though Grace was strong, she trembled among her captors as if she expected to be executed on the spot. Corbin fixed his suit to give himself some time to decide what to do next. He had to be sure and deliberate knowing full well that what he said would be recorded and written down throughout the world.

"Look at her! This is one of the harlots that Satan is using against those who follow the Lord! She defiles herself and forsakes the laws of our God!" Corbin was a little more theatrical than necessary, but his audience was so receptive he decided to go with it. "Shall we shame and denounce her for what she is? Pray for her first that this violent act will persuade her to come back to the fold."

"You and your God do not have any answer and when they find out, I hope they tear you to pieces!" Grace lashed out at Corbin. "I hope they kill you! I hope they kill you and anyone else that follows you."

"She denounces us! It was not I who tried to kill God's messenger!" Corbin looked incredulously at her then turned to the crowds. "Show her our true faith!"

"Glory! Glory! Glory!" The crowd began to chant growing louder as the news cameras moved closer.

"Take her through the streets!" Corbin waved a hand showing his disgust of continuing a discussion. Her use for him was over as he placed a sorrowful look at the camera. "And God help you to see the light. Don't let her hide her shame! Let everyone see the callous murderer she tried to be. Take her away!"

A group of men took her away through the crowd who chanted "Murderer! Harlot!". Some slapped at her while others spat in her face. A police car arrived to take Grace away to the sounds of "Praise God! Praise the Lord!"

Corbin returned to the podium and scanned the audience knowing they were all his and his alone. No one would dare now to question his authority.

"I am confident," Corbin slowly spoke his sheep. "That we will survive the many attacks upon the church as it is our duty to survive. Our God has said that we will be challenged, as I was challenged by that young woman, and mocked by our belief, but do not fear. I am sure that this unexpected event will have a bearing on some of your lives and I hope help you realize the importance of the bill that was passed this week."

Most of the gathering nodded in agreement though none of them had read what was really in the bill itself. If it meant they were safe, it was all that they needed to know.

"We can offer you protection within the church if you follow the rules that have been necessary to be brought before you." Corbin took the opportunity to add to his congregation. "Now if it is in your heart to proclaim your allegiance to the Foundation of the Son of Man, then I suggest you raise your hands while my children hand out selected identifications for each and every one of you. Please to remember that you have to sign your name and number on the registration."

Few refused to take the applications for fear of hearing the wrath of the Archbishop. Some began to walk away so that they did not have to decide.

"Let is sing!" Corbin noticed some leaving. "We will have Dr. James Hart lead us with "Love Is Found in Us All"

Dr. James Hart, second in position to Archbishop John Corbin, had been instrumental in the development of the Foundation of the Son of Man. Hart had served under Joshua and Abraham the highest officials in the Foundation Organization. Hart gets up and smiles to the gathering, lifting his hands to start the singing.

After the song, Corbin returned to the podium to offer a last prayer. As he left, Corbin waded through the crowd shaking hands and giving his blessing. He was thanked for "taking care of a poor sinner with such decency." He finally reached his limo to take him to the Stanton Hotel where he would ready himself for dinner

Chapter Two

"Thank you, John." Corbin accepted a menu from the special waiter authorized to serve him. The hotel had the finest array of food and delicacy in the city. Dr. Hart and two of his trustees sat quietly with him.

After they all ordered, Dr. Hart, a greying man of forty-five with a soft voice that was his trademark in meetings of higher officials, sighed heavily before he spoke.

"It is unbelievable that that woman had the audacity to shoot at you let alone disrupt a great rally." Dr. Hart was disgusted. "It was the largest meeting we ever had. I hope the police," Hart picked up a glass of Port that had been sanctioned by the Foundation at meals and meetings. "do their job because she is both crazy and dangerous like all those Patriots of Christ."

"Well, she's not a threat anymore." Corbin sipped his drink as well. "After the shame I put her through and few years in prison, we can relax a little.

"It might not deter others from trying, yet we got a lot of publicity from it." Dr. Hart leaned back as John brought his steak and fries before him. "I think you did the wisest thing in turning her over to the police."

"Let them get their hands dirty." Corbin salivated over his salmon and fried rice. "We don't want to be known as being unjust to those outside the Foundation."

"We've put off punishment too long." Interjected Irving Greene, Treasurer of the East Coast Children. "We should have tried to disband the Patriots of Christ when they were their weakest two years ago. We had them on murder charges and you, John, stopped us."

"That's right, I did because I told you they would come in handy someday." Corbin nestled a choice piece of salmon on his tongue.

Disgruntled, Greene sat back in his chair staring at orange glazed chicken and vegetables. He waited as usual for his turn to speak. Greene was a small determined man who never found the answer to losing weight on any scale. He had longed for the excitement that had escaped him for forty years. Being sixty-two, he needed to speak as often as possible hoping to be remembered for something in his lifetime.

"I'm glad." Harold Wright, Corbin's Media Coordinator and sometime speech writer which Corbin usually ignored for his own thoughts. "We were given on national news a primary example of what we are fighting against. We need to show strength in following the law that we provided. I think it adds strength to the Foundation."

"I'll speak to Judge Conroe." Corbin tried to ignore the fact Wright was even saying anything, which, of course, he didn't. I'm sure that I can arrange for her to be taken upstate for a rest with her other friends. Those camps have been very useful lately and I'm sure we can work it so the [public will feel sympathy for our cause. However, we will show justification to sending her away for her own safety"

"And ours." Greene threw in.

"We'll reason it this way." Corbin ignored Greene. "That without the basic family unit close together in the Foundation's atmosphere, we can more outrages like tonight. We will explain with the help of consciencious followers we can stop this pitiful plight of our young people who are lost without us."

"Beautiful, John, beautiful." Greene smiled as he took another bite of a biscuit.

"Now let's eat and plan for the arrangements of the services for Joshua in three weeks. "Dr. Hart was more interested in his food than the conversation.

****

Grace was roughly pulled inside the Duffy Square Precinct by two officers did not care about her protests. Grace had a reputation of violence to further the cause of Christ against the Foundation. She had vowed publicly to destroy, through the Patriots of Christ, the Foundation of the Son of Man by any means in freeing the world of their influence.

Grace is brought before detective who recognized her immediately. She had stopped trembling finding her composure before the man who smiled and shook his head.

"What is it this time, Glenn?" the detective asked sitting on top of his desk.

"She took a pot shot at Archbishop Corbin." Glenn sat

her down.

"Technically, I didn't fire a shot….Virginia did and they killed her." Grace stared hard at the detective.

"It doesn't matter." Grace noticed a plaque with the name Gregory Williams on the desk as he spoke. "I'm sure the Archbishop will prefer charges so we'll put you a cell until he does. You'll have to share it with a lunatic in cell four. You won't mind because both of you want to take over the world. You with a gun and him with his mouth. Take her away, Glenn."

"No problem, Greg." Grace smiled at him.

Grace was escorted to cell four and pushed inside where a black man about thirty looked up at her. She noticed he was without shoes yet wearing short with a tie and jacket.

"The two of you can discuss philosophies on revolution together." Glenn sneered at them. "That is, of course, you don't think of something else to do.

The officers laughed as the left them alone. Grace watched to make sure they actually did leave.

"I'm Martin." The black man leaned over offering his hand.

"Don't touch me!" Grace recoiled. "If you're nuts, I'd rather you stay there."

"You really think I'm crazy?" Martin crossed his eyes.

"Why not?" Grace almost laughed.

"Talk to me and find out." Martin leaned back and waited. He had a perfect smile, clean and sounded educated which impressed Grace. If he was really a criminal she couldn't tell.

Grace calmed down enough to sit down across from him. She waited for a while before thinking of what to say.

"I'm sorry, I don't know you." Grace finally spoke to him. "You could be a plant and locked in here to get information from me. It's been a rough day."

"No doubt." Martin stared at her. "I couldn't help but here you tried to kill Corbin?"

"Someone has to do it." Grace smiled at him. His eyes looked kind and his voice measured.

"Are you sure you're fighting for the right reason in the

right way?" Martin glanced down at the floor.

"Yes and no." Grace crossed her legs. "I haven't decided what's right or wrong any more. I'll just do what I think is right."

"Why did you do it?" Martin was just making small conversation.

"I didn't." Grace was matter-of-fact. "I loaded the rifle. Now I will be sent to a camp where I can start all over again."

"An army of hate cannot stop an organization of hate." Martin thought out loud.

"What have you done to stop them?" Grace felt she was talking to wall.

"Love and truth can overcome most anything." Martin waited for her to respond. "They can fight violence with violence, but not love for love."

"You're a member of the Preservation of Christ!" Grace's frustration shocked even Martin.

"It's why they think I'm crazy." Martin folded his arms.

"What are you here for?" Grace demanded.

"For being what I preach." Martin smiled a little. "One full of the Spirit and peace received with a word of affirmation. I had no patience with the Foundation."

"You must be mad or looking to be a martyr which doesn't help any cause." Grace got up to start pacing.

"I want people to realize what it means to be brothers and sisters in the little time that is left." Martin now stared hard at her."

"What's your price for the glory of God?" Grace wanted to be left alone now.

"I am here to tear down the blindness that exists." Martin was so sure of his mission.

"Joshua and Abraham will never let you get away with it." Grace lay on her bed. "You won't get very far at all. They'll cut you down before you can say Amen."

"I will be able to say a thousand Amens before they even think of stopping me." Martin lay down and closed his eyes.

"I'm tired so just leave me alone for the rest of

the night." Grace turned her face to the wall. "Stay in your own bed, too."

"Don't worry." Martin whispered. "I won't be here long. Good night."

Grace fell asleep for a few hours before suddenly wakening to find Martin gone. She jumped up and yelled for the guard who came over to her cell rubbing his eyes.

"Where is he?" Grace demanded.

"Where is who?" the guard was obviously miffed.

"The man who was in here with me." Grace had no patience with him.

"We took him out an hour ago." The guard leaned against the bars. "He was sent upstate and won't bother anyone up there. Whatsamatter? He love ya and leave ya?"

"Take off that smirk and keep out of this cell." Grace looked for something to use in case he decided to come in.

"Sure." He pushed himself away. "But if you want somebody to hold your hand..."

"I'd cut yours off first." Grace listened to the

guard laugh at her as he went back to his chair to sleep. She soon was able to drift off again herself.

When the morning came, the sun did Grace a favor by shining in her face. She awoke to the sound of a key to her cell.

"Come one, beautiful, wake up." Glenn grinned. He was a stocky middle-aged man who was bored with his job. "It's going to be a long trip."

"Where am I going?" Grace worried about being taken out of the cell.

"There's a little place that takes people like you and protects us." Glenn enjoyed telling her what was in store for her. "I'm sure you'll feel right at home with those other lunatics. They think like you do that the world would be a better place if they ran everything."

The guard took Grace by the arm and led her to a waiting fleet of vans with other prisoners of the Foundation. The ride took three hours with Grace unable to watch the scenery till they came to the prison.

The Foundation for Life Penitenciary was one of

twelve prisons reconstructed for political prisoners. It had the designation of Camp Three where Grace was led to the most recent warden, Jack Holcraft, who escorted her into the prison.

"This is Camp Three of the Foundation with a total of seven hundred and five, now seven hundred and six, who have sent here to finish their lives in seclusion." Holcraft recited the same speech he gave to every prison. "In your case you'll be here forever or you'll become a member of the Children of the Son of Man."

"Will that eventually get me released?" Grace already knew the answer.

"We don't like boisterous prisoners, especially women who try to organize groups to disrupt the peace and tranquility of the camp." Holcraft mentally noted that Grace would need to be disciplined. "If you intend to disrupt the peace of this camp there is solitary and then there is the Hole of Tranquility. Solitary is for those who can redeemed and be corrected to the way of the camp. The Hole of Tranquility is a dark place where you can decide the right path if we let you out. Any questions?"

"What are the rules?" Grace just wanted to say something. "As if it really matters."

"That's for you to find out." Holcraft huffed before continuing. "You should join the Children when you have the chance. I was told you are a special case."

"I'm not looking for spiritual damnation." Grace was serious though Holcroft smiled at her. I'm not afraid of what you do to me. You call yourselves followers of God, but you don't know Him."

"I suppose you do." Holcroft was a rather skinny man who enjoyed his position. Grace doubted he even know anything about the Foundation except by their paycheck. "You take a gun to shoot someone and I imagine you believe you are doing a favor for God. The Patriots of God fight against the Children of the Son of Man and who can understand why we are not on the same side?"

"We are not on the same side…." Grace was pulled aside toward the camp courtyard. She was taken to a building for women where disheveled inmates lay on filthy cots.

"Don't give us a reason to put you into solitary." Holcroft whispered. "You may be a celebrity now, but give it a few days and it will wear off."

"I will survive even this." Grace mumbled to herself.

Holcroft and his guards laughed as they turned around and walked away. Grace slumped down on her cot feeling ages older than she was. Four years of guerrilla fighting for the Patriots of Christ left her now with a small barred room and no one to know where she had been taken. Her associates vowed to save her if she was caught. Now she wasn't so sure and a resentment begin to lean on her shoulders. The cause, her cause might just be crumbling in her hands. She fell asleep until the guards woke her to exercise in the courtyard.

It didn't take long to find both old and young milling around the vacant yard. Some looked like their whole family had been taken. Some were talking while others were debating. Others were reading dog-eared books trying to ignore the crying of some of the new prisoners. Grace gravitated to the old and young man who seemed to have a heated debate.

"This camp." The old man was heard. He looked sixty though was probably younger with a streak of sugar white hair on either side. Strains of wrinkles surrounded his eyes as they seem to twinkle as he made his argument. "is one of fifteen in this state holding twenty-two thousand men, women and children. There were some children that were separated from their families to be educated through the Foundation."

"No one knows where they are?" The younger man who did not understand a word the old man was saying and cared less stood sifting on one foot to the other thinking how to get away.

"It's a farce to those who know the truth." The old man noticed Grace coming closer. "Every once in a while they send some clown claiming to be Jesus the Christ trying to dupe those who don't read scripture to join their darn Foundation.":

Grace studied the old man who sounded familiar, but couldn't place where it could have been. She looked up at the guards in the various towers and wondered if escape were possible.

"Who are you?" The old man turned abruptly towards her.

My name is Grace old man." Grace decided to show her tough side.

"I'm Warren and this is Bill who doesn't understand a word I'm saying since he arrived here." Warren patted Bill on the back.

"Wouldn't it be better to get out of here, join the Foundation and with me maybe I can see my wife again." Bill went back to their conversation.

"What happened to your wife?" Grace was interested though Warren was not happy for her to change the subject.

"She was smarter than I was and just joined the Foundation." Bill looked down at his feet. "I just asked what was the Foundation and I ended up here."

"Listen to me!" Warren tried to steer the conversation back to himself. "It's better to ignore them because I don't think the Lord much more with this nonsense. I believe He will be coming soon and I believe a messenger has been sent by Him in this camp right now. He gives us hope and because he doesn't claim to be Christ, I listen to him. The Foundation has sent children and women to distort the message and we've lost a few because of it."

"We can change that." Grace looked hard at Warren. "Can you point out the one who speaks for God?"

"Later." Warren waved his hand. "They're a few undistorted Bibles hidden within the camp. Still there are a few who think Joshua is Christ Himself!"

"I've seen Joshua and his side kick Abraham." Grace say Warren almost jump away from her. "I met Archbishop Corbin who decided our meeting should result in a vacation here."

"You won't make funny jokes soon enough." Bill's face changed enough to have Grace look at him differently. "I need to go."

"You should." Grace watched him quickly disappear in a crowd of men nearby. "He's an infiltrator."

"I know." Warren agreed with a smile. "I try to keep him from the others with long winded arguments."

"You do it well enough." Grace laughed. She thought she might like this old guy if he was the real deal.

"I don't know the day or the hour, but the Lord will come." Warren sighed.

"Until then why don't we unite ourselves and take over the camp?" Grace got right down to business.

"For one thing, there are too many children in the camp and it was done on purpose." Warren already had thought of that. "The second, it would be suicide once out of the camp."

"Really?" Grace wondered.

"There are military groups that move around the forest outside." Warren started to draw in the sand. "Here and here."

"We could get weapons and the men would go out first to subdue them." Grace was sure doing nothing was not an option.

"I already know that a few would not cooperate and would get us all killed." Warren wiped away his drawings as a crowd started to move toward them.

"Time to move on." Warren walked away. "We'll talk again, Grace."

Grace wandered into the gathering crowd who dispersed when Warren walked away. As she walked through the gathering group, Grace listened to various conversations until the dinner sirens sounded. She followed everyone into an auditorium where loudspeakers blared with propaganda. Grace saw the idiocy of it all. When she was finished eating and lead back to her cell, Grace found a bible on a small table next to her bunk.

Grace ignored the sheets and thin pillow to find a window. Looking out she saw Martin from New York pacing back and forth. He stopped suddenly and stared directly into her face.

"You know him?" A young teenager stood next to her.

"I met him in New York." Grace offered only the least information.

"There's a rumor that he's insane." The teenager shook his head. "I don't know, yet."

"Aren't we all insane for being brought here?" Grace watched as Martin came closer to her. Another prisoner came up to him who seemed to be in his forties with a slow gait.

Warren purposely sat on a bench under Grace's window and waited for the man to come to him.

"I'm Jim Connor." The man sat next to Warren. "I need help and I'm told you're the one to talk with."

"What do you want to know?" Warren leaned towards him.

"I don't want to die in here." Jim pleaded more than asked.

"You fear death because you fear the wrath of God." Warren calmly told him. "You both believe and disbelieve at the same time which leads only to your confusion."

"I shake at night thinking that when I die, it'll be just a void of total darkness without sight, without sound and without knowledge that I ever loved." Jim rubbed his hands as if he were cold.

"You'll only continue until you realize that the Lord has concern for you." Warren placed his hand on John's shoulder. "It has been written that he who seeks the Lord will be comforted and none shall be turned away."

"Help me stop the dreams!" John whispered harshly. "I can't stand them any longer. Help me because all I can see is nothing." He began to cry.

"Stop crying!" Warren shook John a little. "Your nightmares will end, but your life won't. Now go back and enjoy the day. Remember when the day comes to stand with me."

"Thank you, Warren!" John felt comforted and quickly left.

Two guards overheard the conversation and came forward as John passed them by. They had smirks on their faces as they stood in front of Warren.

"Playing God now are we?" One of the guards placed his hand on his chin.

"What if he is God, Ted?" Asked the other guard. "I'd hate to upset him."

"He'll zap with you with lightning, Jeff." Ted mocked him. "If you're serious you'll end up sitting there with him."

"No chance of that." Jeff walked away.

Warren sat and stared at Ted who became unnerved and decided to walk away.

****

In the middle of the night a cell door opened as Jeff slipped into Warren's cell. He switched on a flashlight and woke Warren up.

"Wake up!" Jeff nudged Warren.

Warren noticed Jeff was sweating. The guard was a young man in his twenties obviously bored with his job and not sure it could be justified to hold families as prisoners.

"What do you want?" Warren sat up.

"Who do you think you are?" Jeff did not accuse, but was sure there was something else to Warren.

"I can help you overcome your fears." Warren simply said.

"Yes, but who are you?" Jeff was insistent.

"Who do you think I am?" Warren took a deep breath.

"Don't answer my question with a question." Jeff tried hard to keep his voice down.

"Some of them." Jeff nodded toward the other prisoners. "Think you have some divine gift from God."

"But you still fear me, why?" Warren settled back on his cot.

"It's not fear, but confusion because you are here." Jeff looked around hoping not to be seen.

"Why are you here?" Warren asked him watching the nervous tic in Jeff's right eye.

"It's a job that pays well."

"Is it worth it?"

"Better than being dead…or here."

"Do you fear death?" Warren leaned toward Jeff who stepped back against the bars. "What would you die for?"

"My family. My country." Jeff wondered where the conversation was going.

"And what does your family and country promise you after you die?"

"I expect a very good funeral and money for my service."

"So your death would be final?"

"I guess so. I see very few of my relatives walking around." Jeff was nervous about where Warren was leading him.

"There is a way that death is not final." Warren studied Jeff's reaction.

"You are insane if you think you can promise that!" Jeff

kept his voice down. "My talking to you could cost me my job! Do you want to spend time in solitary?"

"I only offer you a way out." Warren knew Jeff would not change.

"Who do you think you are?" Jeff slapped Warren across the face before slamming the cell door. A few other inmates woke up, but ignored the sound.

The prison became quiet except for the soft breeze that filtered through the window. There was a deafening silence that helped Warren to fall asleep.

Chapter Three

"Here at John F. Kennedy Airport, we are giving you live coverage as to the landing of United Airlines jet carrying the leaders of the Foundation of the Son of Man, Joshua and Abraham. Their legend grows as millions follow their every move. This is their first visit to the United States in two years and…." The reporter started toward the jet which drowned out his words.

The bodyguards came out first before Joshua and Abraham made their appearance. A throng of thousands greeted their leaders watching a frail Abraham follow a very robust Joshua. Abraham's appearance matched his personality, one of frail health, undetermined features, but he had a determined stare that unnerved those he met. Everyone knew that Abraham was Joshua's puppet pushing him out front when there is trouble and reel him in when the cameras start to click.

Joshua was the one man in the world, when decisions

were made, that has equated to better relations with all nations. Joshua has foreign powers at his fingertips who have widely invested in the Foundation of the Son of Man. He stood six foot two, square shoulders and full head of hair with a sprinkling of gray which gave him a commanding look at every function.

Both Joshua and Abraham shook hands as they wandered through the crowd while praising them for their act of faith. They refused to ignore any photographer or newsman as they crawled into an awaiting limo. Abraham waved to the crowd with a worried expression before getting inside.

The limo drove them to Park Avenue where a royal suite was awaiting them. They entered the suite after passing by more photographers and reporters where John Corbin and his staff were waiting for them. They looked worried and anxious.

"What's up, John?" Joshua had hoped to relax for a while.

"We're getting a lot friction from the Preservation of Jesus." John held a cache of papers in his hands. "They are recruiting more and more people from the Foundation.

We've tried harassing them with lawsuits, but nothing will stop them. If you have any suggestions, we would love to hear about it."

"Friday night." Joshua pick a carrot from a vegetable tray sitting on a small table. "They're having a concert in Central Park. It has been known protests and outbreaks of fighting have been reported at past events. If such a thing happened there, it would behoove the police to shut it down."

"Wait a minute!" Corbin slap his hands. "Judge Conroe is next door waiting to talk with you. If there is a disruption, he would be the one to sign a restraining order against them."

Corbin ran over to the next room and pulled Judge George K. Conroe, a member of the Bar for twenty-five years and a close associate of Corbin, bringing before Joshua. Conroe was a fifty-two-year old bachelor yet looked thirty-eight though his pronounced stomach did show how well he's earned the respect of the Foundation. He flashed his famous grin as he shook hands with Joshua and Abraham.

"John told me the situation and it can easily be arranged once the disturbance has happened." Conroe tried to keep his official voice steady though he was excited to be amongst the most powerful in the world. "We must protect the public until they can prove their concerts aren't a threat to the peace and comfort of the city."

"Very good, George." Joshua admired the efficiency that Conroe always brought to the Foundation. "John knows a group that is dependable and loyal to the Foundation. We have no room for these heretics. Better yet,,,"

Joshua suddenly walks away from the group and picks up a cell phone and calls as everyone else stands mute.

"Hello? Brother Michael?" Joshua was always impatient when he wanted things to get done. "This is Joshua. I'd like a favor from you. This is the situation, Friday night is a big event for the Preservation of Jesus. Since I'm in town we need peace and unity." A pause. "All right then, we understand each other." Another pause. "God bless you, too."

"Okay, gentlemen." Joshua took a deep breath before rejoining the group. "It's set for Friday night and the good news will be on the eleven o'clock news."

"There won't be any real violence?" Abraham was not happy with the decision.

"Abraham." Joshua was very condescending to him.

"Trust me. Whatever happens is god sent and you know as well as I do, the future is no longer in our hands."

"It's in our best interests." Corbin needed to show his allegiance to Joshua. "This weekend will be big and I have to go make preparations for all of you."

The others in the room took their cue from Corbin as they all left leaving Joshua and Abraham to themselves.

"Abe." Joshua sternly talked to Abraham as a disappointed father. "I don't like to be questioned in front of those under my supervision. If you have to question me, wait until they have left the room. You should know better by now."

Abraham sat down a soft lounge chair while Joshua moved to his room to get ready for the coming weekend.

****

"Good evening ladies and gentlemen." Andrea Wilson smiled broadly into the camera. She was a thirty-five-year old blonde who was one of the few announcers who deserved her position. "Here in Central Park the rock group

Righteous Thunder will perform to a crowd of over one hundred thousand fans. It is a concert sponsored by the Preservation of Jesus. Earlier this year this group was part of the Patriots for Christ singing songs against the Foundation."

The crowd started to applaud as the Righteous Thunder walked onto the stage.

"Tonight we will see if anything has changed in their music and message." Andrea almost sounded like a fan of the group. "They mentioned that they want to bring about a new spirit and a new mind. Security seems to be less than minimal with such a huge gathering. We will show complete coverage at eleven o'clock news. Now back to George Connor." Andrea smiled until the cameras turned off.

People started coming closer to the stage which was a twenty-five platform six feet off the ground. There were fifteen speakers around either side of a set of drums facing out toward the audience. Some within the audience were singing. Laughing and discussing past concerts. The emcee approached a microphone, raised his hands to quiet down those who had their backs turned.

"If you people will settle down and be patient." The Emcee who was a thirty-year-old pastor that put the program together. "We'll start the concert in a few minutes."

Just before Righteous Thunder came on stage there was the whining of motorcycles through the park entrance. Fifteen riders dismounted forcing themselves through the crowd. After some curious looks most of the audience ignored the disturbance and turned back to the stage. The Emcee returned to the microphone smiling broadly.

"Tonight." The Emcee began. "We are bringing the most popular band in America. They have been subject to controversy ever they rededicated their lives to Jesus the Christ. They have spread the Word all over the country through their music. Let's have a warm welcome to Righteous Thunder."

On stage came the band to mounting applause and shouts of approval. Righteous Thunder was composed of four guys and a girl. The girl, Barbara Challey, approached the microphone. Challey was the spokesperson and lead singer.

"The first song we want to sing for you was a hit before our rededication." Challey looked over the crowd. "We did not know our God and how intimate we could be with Jesus.

The song is "Come and Tell Me." A song written before we devoted ourselves to Christ.

    Challey grabbed the microphone as the band started the instrumental.

"Come and tell when
and then tell me why.
I feel the pain
of nothing in my mind.

People listening for nothing
expecting a great new dawn,
using mechanical energy
to take the loneliness away.

Come and tell me who,
Come and show me how
to take this hanging dream
from my red-streaked eyes.

Bring the last dead cup
of the leftover wine,
pull out the choking hate,
sew up the broken lies.

I want to see the life
flow into my veins,

see the reasons for it
to run so far away.

Come and tell me now,
Come and let me know,
why speak of ever love
if it's never seen around.

Come and tell me when,
Can't you tell me why?
Come and tell me who,
Can't you tell me how?"

As the last notes were played, the crowd started to applaud and the sound resounded throughout the park. The group of motorcyclists got up during the ovation and made their way toward the stage. One of the men carried an elongated case on his back while the others kept their hands in their pockets.

"We have a new song." Challey continued wiping the sweat on her forehead from the lights with a small towel. "That will be sung for the first time in a public performance. It's called 'Plastic Thunder".

"Plastic Thunder!
I was hit by plastic lightning
by all the plastic leaders,
killing all my hopes and dreams,
but Jesus told me it was only
Plastic Thunder!

Why, oh why the plastic charade?
Why, oh why must we constantly play
with everyone's life this way?
Must we be so far removed
and destroyed by useless rage?
Plastic Thunder!

I hear those plastic people
call all their plastic children
to see their plastic money
and read their plastic bible.
Plastic Thunder!"

Challey slowed the pace of the music that started to build as a storm. She was almost crying before she began to sing again.

"Floating on the water
with my face to the sky,
I saw people waving to me

knowing I knew He died for me.
Jesus Thunder!

Watching and walking
to the path of stones
where God is waiting still
looking for my hand to guide.
Jesus Thunder!

I hear my Lord calling me.
I see Him coming my way.
It's Jesus, He is with me
and with you if you stay.
Jesus Thunder!
Jesus thunder!"

Challey waited for the applause to stop when she saw the group of motorcyclists in front of her. They were not applauding.

"We're here tonight. "Challey tried to ignore them. "Not only as ones to show you the way through Christ, but also to tell you that you are being deceived by some who call themselves men of God. You never hear the word of Jesus unless necessary. The real Jesus is Spirit not walking in flesh and blood and certainly not dictating our lives. Jesus is our savior not...." Challey was interrupted as the man with the long case opened it, took out a rifle and shot her in the chest.

"They've got guns!" The audience shouted near them. "Run!"

The other motorcyclists pulled out guns and started shooting. Three more fell from the shots.

"My God! They're killing us!" Another woman cried as she tried to escape.

"Don't shoot! Don't shoot!" Two men stood in the way of the shooters. "We'll do anything, anything just don't kill us! Please!"

The two men fell dead as more shots rang out. A knife flew out of the crowd hitting the man with the rifle. The shooters pushed their way through the panic toward their motorcycles firing at anyone close by. Band members stood around Challey who was dying with the microphone in her hand.

Some the men in the crowd turned and jumped on two of the bikers, but were shot in the back by their friends. One of the bikers jumped on the stage and shot the drummer and lead guitarist before running back to his bike. Sirens are heard as the bikers sped off through the chaos.

When the police arrived, they saw that around twenty people had fallen dead or wounded. Screams came from the injured in front of the stage. Endless crying and screaming.

"Lord Jesus! Help us! Forgive them!" The lead guitarist held his side.

"I can't believe this!" One of the policemen shook his head.

"Maniacs." Mumbled another.

"Anyone call an ambulance?" A third called out.

"At least ten dead, twenty wounded." The first policeman tried to make sense of it all.

"Jerry! Jerry! They've killed my husband a woman cried out from the front of the stage.

"My dear God! Why? Why?" A voice from the far end of the park was heard.

Minutes later the area was under control with five ambulances and twelve medical advisors tending the wounded.

"Are those reporters?" A Sergeant was annoyed. "Tell them if they take one picture. I'll arrest them! Then I'll burn their cameras. Keep everyone away who is not here to help."

Sirens continued to pierce the air off and on as peace slowly encompassed the park.

****

"Why don't you put the news on, Abe?" Joshua sat down comfortably in his leather chair.

Abraham picked up the remote and started to channel surf. Finding the right station, Abraham settled back waiting for the commercials to end.

"Good evening ladies and gentlemen." Emma Coast kept a smile as she began to tragic news. "A special report from Central Park showed a riot ensued during the concert by Thunder. Thunder was promoted by the Preservation of Jesus and was warned of threats against them. Thirteen are dead including lead singer Challey of Thunder. Many were wounded, but expected to live. At Central Park is George Connor who will tell us what happened."

"This is George Connor in Central Park where a mass shooting occurred claiming the lives of thirteen men and women with twenty or more wounded. Eyewitnesses said some of the crowd objected to a group of motorcyclists blocking the stage where Thunder was performing. They weren't sure who started the fight, but guns were quickly drawn and the melee began. Next to me is a witness to the fighting."

"Well, like I told the police." An eighteen-year-old nervously scratched his cheek as he spoke. "I was standing next to these guys who seemed to be enjoying the concert when some guy jumped one of them with a knife. The guy with the knife was holding a Bible as he stabbed blindly at them saying "Jesus love you!" One of the bikers pulled a gun and shot him. Then the crowd went crazy trying to attack the bikers and they just defended themselves."

"Well, thank you for clearing that up for us." Connor patted the shoulder of the man. "I'm sure you're glad to be alive to tell your story."

"I sure am." The teenager looked into the camera and smiled broadly.

"Now back to our studio." Connor nudged the man from his spot. "Emma?"

The cameras closed in on Emma as adjusted herself in her seat.

"The Preservation of Jesus tried to explain why the riot began, but no witness has come forward that would explain who was behind the fighting." Emma brushed away her blond wisps that fell over her eyes. "Rumors that a new holy war might begin because of this event, but that is only rumor which the Foundation has assured us. Again the group Thunder was performing at the time where lead singer Challey was killed and lead guitarist, George Hamden, died on the way to the hospital. No arrests were made, but an investigation is pending. This will definitely keep future concerts from the Preservation of Jesus from continuing in Central Park. In other news...."

Abraham sat open mouthed as he listened to the report. He then looked over at Joshua in disbelief.

"I think….." Joshua thought for a second. "The Preservation of Jesus will think twice before having any other meetings in the park. What about you, Abe? By the way, turn that thing off."

"I don't like the way this was done." Abraham turned off the television. "It will lead to more trouble than we might be able to handle. I didn't think there would be a massacre."

"Don't worry, Abe." Joshua was condescending, but

reassuring. "There's no way they can trace it back to us. Even if it did, our media will sugar coat it. I hope you're not getting soft, Abe. We have little room to be soft and forgiving. You do understand that, right?"

"Don't worry, Josh." Abraham settled back in his chair. "I worked too hard for the Foundation to let it down…or you."

"That's good, Abe" Joshua smiled, but his eyes narrowed just a little. "I'd hate to have our friendship questioned over such a little thing."

Joshua got up to make a snack in the kitchen while Abraham turned the television on again with the sound down. Two rooms now divided the once united prophets.

Chapter Four

An old Chevy pulled up to Harvey's Restaurant in Orangeburg, New York. John Wise and Karl Avery got out of the car and headed inside. John was thirty-two, a mastermind in extortion, theft and kidnapping while Karl was a sniper for the Patriots of Christ. They had been partners for six months, but John was not impressed with his partner.

They dressed in business suits giving anyone the impression they were part of the Foundation. Inside Harvey's were a few young and middle-aged couples who never looked up at them. John asked for a booth as a waitress directed them near the back.

"If we're supposed to talk business." Karl was annoyed at how public that became. "The why go to a place so public?

"Because." John was already irritated with him. "I want people to see us in case something goes wrong. I want no trouble till we start it."

"What's up then?" Karl spoke as low as he could. Karl turned forty and trusted no one, even his partner. He usually worked alone which made him safer.

John hesitated as their waitress came back to get their order and placed two glasses of water in front of them. Karl shook his head telling her to come back later.

"I've been told to get rid of Joshua and Abraham by next week." John watched Karl's eyes widen in surprise." They're planning an appearance outside the Hilton the day after tomorrow. I thought about a bomb, but their security is pretty good. Two rifles across the street can keep us from missing them both."

"You picked a lousy place to plan a job." Karl was upset. "What were you thinking?"

"No one cares." John waved him off.

"We better be getting paid enough to knock off two of the most powerful men in the world." Karl looked around as he spoke.

"It'll work out." John sat back and sipped his water.

"Besides, we have tickets to Canada afterwards."

"If it all works out." Karl shook his head.

The waitress came back to take their order as John smiled at her. He planned to leave a big enough tip so she would remember them.

****

Grace waited patiently in her cell for the guard to let her out for the afternoon exercise. When she was let out, she wandered around listening the many groups of inmates talking. As she came closer to one of the bigger crowds, she realized they surrounded Warren.

"The time is coming." Warren sat comfortably on a bench, speaking to a gathering of twelve listeners. "When your Lord will come as a thief in the night. Too many frauds use his name to condone murder, fornication, drunkenness and war. Even here we fight amongst ourselves about the Word of God."

"And who are you to tell us this?" A young woman who folded her arms defiantly stood in front of him.

"The mark of the beast is coming." Warren looked into her eyes. "The fact that none of you have that mark is why you will never leave here. When it comes it will be a symbol of Satan that will bring hardship, condemnation and despair. You asked who I was to speak to you in this way and I say the Lord sent me to bring you strength and peace. Do not fight amongst yourselves about simple things. Know that God is watching over you."

A guard passing by was listening to Warren and became concerned.

"Hello, Burt." Warren saw the surprise on his face.

"I want you to break this up." Burt forced him to the front. He was a stocky man with no religious views just needed to keep his job. "I'll have to put you in solitary if you continue to incite the inmates."

"You cannot lock up the truth." Warren stood up and smiled at him. "You will have to choose someday who it is to place your trust in."

"I trust in this stick on your head!" Burt was unnerved by Warren. "No more backtalk!"

"My apologies, Burt." Warren sat down again.

Burt had the urge to use his club, but seeing the inmates around him decided against it.

"Get back to your cells. All of you!" Burt wasn't going to take any chances. "And forget about dinner tonight! This man is insane and he is here as an enemy of society and the state."

Grace stared blankly at Burt before walking away. She passed an old man who was laughing to himself.

"What's so funny?" Grace asked him. The old man had laughing eyes and years of wrinkles.

"Warren must be insane." The old man winced in pain. "If he were from God, he wouldn't be stuck in this dungeon like the rest of us. By the way, my name is Graddie."

"I'm Grace." She held out her hand which he didn't shake. "I think maybe he would, prophet or not."

"You're the one that preaches violence and revolution." Graddie stared hard at her. "Now you stand up for someone who doesn't agree with you. Don't stand too close to him or you'll starve."

Graddie walked away from her in a slow gait. Grace continued on to her cell feeling more alive than ever. She didn't understand why, but it was a good feeling.

Two hours later all the inmates got their meals anyway because of the rumors of rebellion that circulated. Grace looked over the cafeteria for a place to sit when she saw Warren siting by himself. Grace decided to sit with him, no she felt compelled to sit with him.

"All right to sit down with you?" Grace had already decided to sit down.

"Do you understand why you stood up for me?" Warren started the conversation.

"How did you know I did at all?" Grace was almost surprised.

"I heard you." Warren took a bite of bread. "I am here for you."

"I don't know why I did." Grace was puzzled, but gave him the benefit of the doubt. "At times I think you're crazy and then I wonder."

"Nobody is sure of themselves." Warren sipped on a cup of water. "Without trust or faith what one says, what one does and why one does it. I bring the message of love, life and trust. I am not here to judge you. You, however, worry about the judgement of those around you.

"I'm unnerved about who you might be." Grace felt relaxed around Warren.

"You don't have to sit with me." Warren could tell she wanted to move away.

Grace moved to a table away from Warren. One of the more burly inmates walked over to her and sat down. He had scars on his face from fighting, but did not sit to threaten her.

"Has that guy been bothering you?" He said leaning close to Grace. "If he has, I'll fix it so he doesn't bother you again."

"No, he hasn't been bothering me." Grace appreciated his concern. "He does mean well and I doubt if he would hurt anyone intentionally."

"Don't tell me you trust him?" He smiled to himself. "I think he's a con man and crazy to boot. I wouldn't be on his side if anything comes down from the guards. There is talk."

"What do you mean?" Grace tried not to sound surprised.

"Never mind." He saw something in her eyes that made him hesitate. "I don't think you understand."

He pushed himself away from the table letting Grace finish her meal before going back to her cell. She wondered where Warren went and what was she going to do. What she was sure of was that she had to escape.

Chapter Five

"John?" Karl called wondering what to do next. "We've been here six hours and they are two hours late."

"Quit complaining and stay off the phone!" John was thinking of shooting him.

John was getting anxious, too as he shifted positions a few times already. They both carried Weatherbye .308 rifles with scopes mounted on small stands. John wondered how long before they would be spotted. Reporters surrounded the Hilton waiting for the two prophets which told John they would only get one chance to get a clear shot.

"Here they come." Karl told himself.

"You've got Abraham." John whispered into his phone.

Karl readied his rifle looking through the scope as the limo carrying Joshua and Abraham pulled outside the entrance. Abraham was the first to get out, but Joshua hesitated.

"John, he'll get away if I don't shoot now." Karl was impatient.

"Hold up." John told him.

Joshua started to get out of the limo when the shot rang out and Abraham fell to the ground. John fired two shots that seemed to miss Joshua who fell back into the limo.

"Why didn't you wait!" John was furious as he picked up his rifle and ran.

"He would've gotten away!" Karl raced behind him.

"You stupid…" John disappeared down a flight of stairs to the alley behind.

"Somebody call an ambulance." One of Joshua's guards shouted. "Joshua is still alive!"

"Somebody help our saviors!" A woman in the crowd cried out in anguish.

"God be merciful to one of our own!" An older man crept closer to see Abraham on the ground bleeding.

Newsmen with their cameras swarmed around the body of Abraham and asking those in the crowd how they felt about what had happened. Close-ups of the wounded Joshua were taken just before his limo sped away.

"Fifteen minutes ago." William Hoffman from JKLM news stood in front of a portable monitor. "At least two snipers shot and killed Abraham while wounding Joshua as they got out of their limousine in front of the Hilton. Abraham was one of the founders of the Foundation of the Children of Men. Joshua is now on his way to St. Mary's Hospital to undergo emergency surgery."

Yelling and screaming interrupted his commentary which had Hoffman turn his monitor towards the noise. A few in the crowd were pointing across the street and screaming that they saw someone. Then when Hoffman turned the monitor across the street could only find a few police officers searching the rooftops.

"There are reports that one of the snipers was killed by his confederate." Hoffman related a rumor that was circulating. "If true, we don't know officially if a sniper is dead. We will continue coverage of this gruesome scene…. Just a minute! Here comes Sergeant Parker of the New York City Police Department. Maybe he can tell us more of what has happened and the physical state OF Joshua who is undergoing surgery as we speak. Excuse me Sergeant Parker, I'd like to ask you a few questions if you don't mind."

Sergeant Parker continued walked on by and ignored Hoffman without a second look.

"Tell us what condition would you say Joshua was in when he was taken to the hospital?" Hoffman followed Parker who turned to face him.

"Joshua took two bullets in the chest and side." Sergeant Parker gave a short statement. "Abraham took a bullet to the head and was killed instantly. We're looking for the other man or men involved. That should answer any questions for now so excuse me I've got a job to do."

Sergeant Parker walked inside the Hilton and warned Hoffman not to follow him in.

"Until we have further information we return you to our regularly scheduled program which is still in progress." Hoffman then picked up his monitor and wandered around hoping to find out anything that would get him back on the air.

****

Joshua was rushed through to St. Mary's halls to the operating room while John Corbin, Jim Hart and twenty special police to guard the intensive care unit Joshua would end up after being operating on.

Newsmen were scattered inside and out of the building blocking other patients waiting for help. For hours, doctors worked on Joshua who was suffering from two bullets lodged near his heart and his right lung. Doctors were bombarded with questions whether they had anything to do with saving Joshua or not. Finally, one doctor emerged and raised his hands to quiet the reporters.

"Gentlemen." The head surgeon, Alexander Granzky, addressed their concerns. "I know you're anxious to know of Joshua's condition. It is my duty to inform you that he is in a coma and has a slim chance to survive. We will hope for the best. He was shot just below the heart and through the right lung. We were able to stabilize his condition so do not be discouraged and let God be with him at this point."

"What are you planning to do if Joshua gets worse?" A reporter blurted out. "Is it possible to save him at all?"

Could you tell us how the operation went in detail?"

Another reporter called out. "How much damage was done?"

The doctors walked off leaving the reporters behind even as they still asked questions. Cell phones abounded as they called their editors giving what little they knew for the next edition.

Archbishop Corbin arrived at the hospital which started a new round of murmuring that Joshua was near death. He refused questions as he went straight to the intensive care center.

"We don't want to be disturbed." Corbin instructed the guards in front of Joshua's room.

As he went in, the halls were cleared except for the guards. There is dead silence except for soft murmurings behind the door. Corbin spends half the night with Joshua praying for Joshua's recovery without results. After six hours, Corbin came out and returned to his limo to leave.

In the morning, a nurse enters Joshua's room finding him sitting up and staring her way. He was writing on a pad of paper bemused that she was speechless.

"What do you think you're doing?" The nurse was not sure what to do. "You shouldn't be sitting up in your condition."

"And what condition is that?" Joshua smiled.

"I'd better get the doctor." She says while leaving and hurried down the hall looking for any doctor to come with her. She came back with three doctors almost as fast as she left the room.

"Please lie down." Granzky insisted Joshua listen to him. "We need to evaluate your condition."

"Fine." Joshua was impatient. "I feel good. I need to let my people that I'm alive and well."

Joshua was given a complete examination and other than the scars of the operation, Joshua seemed healed. There was no reasonable explanation to attest to the fact that Joshua was no longer in danger. Archbishop Corbin was notified and raced back to the hospital. Standing outside, Corbin addressed the reporters.

"It can only be explained as a miracle!" Corbin raised his hands in triumph.

Two hours later, Joshua meet reporters at the Hilton lounge which was packed with camera crews and reporters anxious to ask about the miracle. Joshua approached a bevy of microphones and recorders to meet the inevitable barrage of questions that would be thrown at him.

"Before you ask any questions." Joshua struggled a little adjusting himself in a wooden chair. "I would like to make a statement as to the.... as to my recent recovery. My Lord has seen fit that I should live to continue my work in this nation and the world. The healing I have gone through is a sign of the power of my God and I can see no point of this healing, this miracle other than to present to you a new messiah. To prove that there is hope and power that I can bring to all of you."

"Isn't it so that your life is still in danger?" one reporter asked.

"That may be true, but as you can see I am protected by a higher force." Joshua stood up and pulled off his shirt to show the bullet wounds he had taken. He then replaced his shirt before continuing. "I now have no fear of death from any side because my God has healed me and I will fulfill my purpose on this earth."

"Are you that certain?" Another reporter asked.

"I have assurance that my time is not yet here." Joshua became more animated.

"What about your plans for Times Square?" William Hoffman finally was able to make his way to the front. "Are your services going to continue even after the death of Abraham?"

"Of all people, Abraham would want me to continue in those services as the Foundation is more important than any individual." Joshua began to show irritation with the reporters. "It would be unnecessary to discontinue anything because I am sure Abraham would do the same if our roles were reversed. We will remember him in our service, but the Foundation is bigger than any of us."

"Do you know who tried to kill you?" Hoffman asked.

"No, I do not understand who would try to do such a thing." Joshua thought the answer should be obvious. "I am a peaceful man, a loving man. I've hurt no one in my life. What motive could they possibly have?"

"There's talk of you being the new prophet, a messiah who will save this world." A young reporter fawned over Joshua. "I wonder if you embrace that view or deny it flatly?"

"I am called a prophet, but a messiah…" Joshua hesitated purposely as if he never considered it. "A messiah infers I am self-aware of it. You decide."

"Do you have any thought as to the successor for Abraham?" Hoffman asked the question everyone else thought might have been too soon.

"I can't answer that question right now." Joshua appreciated the question. "We have a funeral to deal with and a great rally ahead of us."

Joshua walked to a side door and left the reporters behind to mull around. Archbishop Corbin patiently waited for Joshua at the elevator. After the entered, Joshua changed his smile to a serious sigh.

"Who was the fool that shot me?" Joshua inferred Corbin find out.

"We don't know yet." Corbin had nothing to give him. "Some say the Patriots of Christ had something to do with it."

"Find them and then we'll take care of the Patriots later." Joshua was impatient. The fools were supposed to take care of Abraham and only make an attempt on my life. They almost killed me."

Corbin and Joshua quietly finished the trip up to their rooms. Corbin was cautious not to upset Joshua unless he wanted to be next.

Chapter Six

"Here we are ladies and gentlemen." Arthur Wilson was given primary reporter following at a riot in Camp Three. "We are at Camp Three just above Albany, New York. For the last two hours, the inmates held themselves in the camp's cafeteria. They have made numerous demands such as better clothing, food, hospitalization and housing. A strange request they are making is for the removal of a man called Warren who, they say, is disrupting the camp. "

The sound of shouting interrupted Wilson until he realized there was nothing going on.

"I am sure the state will be able to secure order at the camp in time to save the hostages." Wilson was just filling time since he had no idea what was going to happen. "We will give you further details as information gets to us for the six o'clock news."

Inside the camp, the guards have the cafeteria

surrounded trying to negotiate with them. Two men who represented the other inmates discussed the demands that they wanted met. Grace and Warren stood in the back of the room waiting for the insanity to stop.

"If you are someone special, do something to stop this." One of the inmates confronted Warren.

"Nothing I say or do will convince you or anyone else that what is happening will only get worse." Warren leaned against the wall. "The light will come soon enough."

"Are you people crazy?" Grace stood in front of Warren.

"Shut up!" The inmate slapped Grace. "This is the last time you defend him!"

Outside the building, the guards were becoming impatient. A couple left to speak to the media and Holcroft about the progress.

"Well?" Holcroft hoped there was good news.

All they really seem to be concerned about is getting two inmates out of the camp." The guards responded.

"And who are they?" Holcroft thought it was crazy to cause so much trouble over two inmates.

"The guy Warren and his new friend Grace." They shrugged.

"Is it that lunatic from New York City?" Holcroft knew who he was.

"I think so." Was one of the guard's answer. "He's being held inside as a gun shield and the girl stands with him. They want an answer in an hour. They have two of our own in there and will send them out piece by piece if we don't comply."

"If I take them out of there, they might demand something more." Holcroft tried to think of another solution. "No other camp will have him."

"What about the governor?" The guard asked.

Before Holcroft could answer, a helicopter fly overhead landing in a field near the camp. He wondered what new problem had arrived. As he walked over to his office, Joshua and Archbishop Corbin confronted him along with Jim Hart. They shook hands before Holcroft spoke first.

"I didn't expect to see you here, sir." Holcroft nearly bowed.

"I get the impression you might need some help." Joshua looked behind him. "Since it unusual to have one man cause such a problem, I had to find out who he was. Perhaps, the Foundation can help you."

"This is a simple problem which should be resolved soon." Holcroft didn't believe what he was saying. "The thing is that the inmates are willing to fight to get rid of him. We have seven hundred inmates here who think he is a lunatic."

"I understand that." Joshua stopped him. "I was briefed by my aides that he thinks he's a prophet of some kind for the Preservation of Jesus. So I have a solution however that will be of little risk to you and great benefit to me."

"Right now I can use all the suggestions you can give." Holcroft wanted to get the camp back to normal.

"Release him." Joshua looked into the surprised face of Holcroft. "Now before you say it's impossible, the governor has signed off on it. I gave him my reasons, but trust me about this. You won't regret it."

"Well, if the governor approved, I'll agree to it." Holcroft tried not to show his relief even though he instantly pulled out his cell phone.

"Tell the inmates we will take Warren out of the camp." Holcroft ordered the coordinator to end the siege.

"We'll concede food and better housing for an added incentive to get back our camp."

Within the hour, Warren was taken away and the inmates were escorted back to their cells. They watched as Warren was handcuffed and brought to Holcroft's office.

"What's going to happen to him?" A young inmate cried out.

"He's being released." One of the guards mistakenly told the truth.

"That's not fair!" Some of the inmates stopped to protest.

"You wanted him out of your sight." The guard almost laughed. "You got what you wanted so get back to your cells."

Grace looked into the eyes of warren was staring at her as he mouthed the words "See you on the outside." Confused she was pushed inside her building. Warren was brought to Holcroft who was standing before Joshua and the others.

"Tell me." Joshua began without introduction. "What concerns you most?"

"That you will win the battle though we both know

that won't happen." Warren rubbed his wrists after he was set free.

"What is he talking about?" Corbin saw the way they looked at each other.

"It means…" Joshua was aware of his adversary. "He's no saint or threat to me."

"You know what I really mean." Warren stared hard at Joshua who never once worried about what he said.

"I might know, but I have no choice except to continue my work." Joshua's eyes flared red that only Warren saw. ":I intend to make it interesting no matter the outcome."

Warren stood for a few moments without saying a word and nothing was said by Joshua who turned his back on him. Corbin and the others wondered what was going on.

"Take him away." Joshua waved Warren away.

After Warren was released, Joshua instructed everyone out except Corbin. The confusion was on everyone's face except Joshua.

"So what are we going to do with him?" Corbin was disgusted with what had happened and wondered what was going on through his head.

"We are going to use him to suit a very definite purpose." Joshua wondered how much to tell Corbin. "He is going to be our bread and butter in the near future because of the special publicity he will get. I'm sure he will eventually fall and we will pick him up."

"What do you mean?" Corbin was puzzled.

"He is going to speak against me and soon he will be labeled insane." Joshua already was thinking of what he could do. "Everyone will realize how powerful the Foundation really is. We will prove him to be the Anti-Christ and destroy all those who follow him. Justification! Justification!"

"That's a big chance to take." Corbin was not so sure. "What if it doesn't work?"

"If it does work, the Foundation will solidify its position throughout the world." Joshua was so sure of the future results.

"I am with you, Joshua." Corbin became excited, too.

"I thought you would see the light, John." Joshua couldn't care less if Corbin stayed or was left behind.

"How can we proceed?" Corbin rubbed his hands together. "What can I do?"

"We must let every news outlet in the world know who this man claims he is." Joshua laughed at his own idea that seemed to flow freely. "We have to mold public opinion to suit our needs and then let the press will take it from there. When we get to Times Square, we will have the greatest audience ever amassed in one place."

"There are reporters outside waiting for you to speak with them." Corbin started toward the door.

"I'll start the ball rolling then?" Joshua enjoyed Corbin's enthusiasm.

"Maybe it should come from me." Corbin stopped suddenly. "They might think something was not right if you lowered yourself to speak about this man… Warren? Is it?"

"Okay John." Joshua got up and left for his helicopter while Corbin addressed the reporters.

The hordes of reporters were bursting with questions. Some wondered why Joshua had left Corbin by himself.

"I am here." Corbin began looking at each one of them as he spoke. "To make a statement on behalf of Joshua and

Captain Holcroft. The reason we have released the inmate called Warren is that he claims to be a prophet on the same level as Joshua. He could be insane, but the only way to know is allow you to judge him."

"This is the first time we've heard of this man." A reporter near Corbin raised his hands in surrender. "Who is he? Why are you giving him to us?"

"He infers that he is special." Corbin just winged whatever came to mind. "He could be dangerous or maybe not. Joshua will deal with the issue when we meet in Times Square. Find out what he stands for. Now I have to join Joshua in New York City. Thank you for your time."

Corbin walked away from the reporters who cried out for clarification. He shunned their protests and entered a waiting limo which quickly sped away.

Chapter Seven

Grace lay on her bed resting in thought upon the day's events. She felt lucky that she wasn't hurt though she saw the angry looks from her cellmates. Grace's train of thought was broken with the sound of footprints that stopped outside her cell. When she looked, she saw Holcroft glaring down at her.

"We need to talk." Holcroft opened the cell door and walked her outside without guards.

"About what?" Grace hesitated to follow him.

"It's about Warren." Holcroft insisted she follow him.

"Why do you want to talk with me about him?" Grace felt a chill creep up her spine. "I'm like everyone else."

"No, you're not." Holcroft ignored her protest.

"All right." Grace gave in.

They walked in silence to Holcroft's office passing purposely many of the inmates that caused the riot. When they got to the office twenty inmates stood in front of the building. Inside, Grace sat down as Holcroft leaned against his desk. There were no guards in the office or outside the office.

"We were told that you were the leader that caused the riot." Holcroft looked hard at her.

"What!" Grace almost jumped to her feet, but instead tensely held on the edge of her chair.

"I told you what would happen if you started any trouble here." Holcroft noticed Grace was angry. "Now just sit there and listen. You can rant and rave all you want, however, we were told you were the brains behind a committee setting up the demands and threats by the inmates."

Grace gritted her teeth expecting a firing squad to take her away.

"It has come to my attention that if we do not do something about this now, more outbreaks of civil disobedience." Holcroft walked around and sat at his desk. "It is quite evident that we have no alternative, but put you into solitary. Maybe a couple of days there will alter your thoughts about adhering to our way of life. I hope you don't mind the rats and spiders since nothing has been done to clean up after the last ten inmates sent there."

"Are you crazy?" Grace finally stood up to confront him. "How could I have gotten the backing of those idiots so soon?"

"I don't keep up with everything that goes on here." Holcroft leaned back in his chair. "For all I know you were sent here to cause disturbances and maybe break someone out of this camp."

"You know better." Grace noticed Holcroft pushing a button under his desk. Two guards came in and waited for orders.

"Take her out and show her our guest room." Holcroft turned toward his window while she was pulled out of the room.

Grace was taken to solitary building that held six cells set apart from the main area. She was shoved inside a six by eight room without a window or light except the small rays that shown through the main door. The guards threw a small stick to keep the rats away.

One guard was assigned to the main door. He smiled to

himself when he heard Grace scream and shake the cell door to escape the rats. Most of the night the rats terrified Grace until complete exhaustion forced her on the moldy mattress on the floor.

****

Three days later, outside, a number of inmates gathered still talking about Grace and Warren. As Grace was released, she attempted to hold herself up from the exhausting siege from the rats. No one helped her as she ventured toward the showers to clean the filth on her. She must have felt twice her age knowing her hair was a mess and the tired look in her eyes.

"How did it go, beautiful?" A mocking voice seemed to slap her in the face.

"Did you bring us any souvenirs?" Another voice laughed at her.

"Your friend walked out on you." A woman's voice whispered as a crowd began to gather. "what do you think of him now?"

"I…stand…with him." Grace stammered.

"Why you little …" A heavy set balding man picked up a rock and threw it at her hitting her shoulder.

Grace went down quickly to the ground while two more threw stones at her. She lay unconscious on the ground while the inmates disbanded. Two guards picked her up and took her to the infirmary.

****

"It's only been twenty-four hours since Warren had been released from camp." Arthur Wilson was hoping for an interview. "He has been drawing large crowds wherever he goes, but more out of curiosity than substance. We now take you to taped segment from this morning in Corning, New York."

The tape shows Warren with twelve individuals behind him and a large gathering in front. Some newsmen are around the outskirts looking bored.

"We need to know who you are here and if you intend to cause trouble?" Mayor Jeri Armstrong was concerned she may have to deal with violence in her town. "Why did they release you?"

"I am just passing through." Warren told her the truth. "Is it so important who I am or what I have to say to you? Who I am is up to you, but I am not Him you seek. If you believe in what you have read and what has been said, then the truth should fill the yearnings in your soul. The time is coming soon enough where love and patience would soon wear out. The Lord gave you life and do you repay him with rebellion and worship another?"

"There are rumors that the woman, Grace, who supported you has been attacked?" Mayor Armstrong stood closer to Warren.

"Yes and I will see her soon." Warren saw Armstrong's confusion.

"I've heard she's in solitary." Armstrong watched Warren closely.

"Not for long." Warren smiled at her.

"What is your opinion of Joshua?" The media represented by Antonia Wilkins interrupted Armstrong.

A time is coming when you will shout out 'It is he! It is

him! But you will not realize that you are blind to the teachings of Christ." Warren watched as some of the crowd gasped. "At that time, you will lead yourselves to your own destruction as a false prophet will come before you and declare himself God. You will laud yourselves and honor him, you will bear the mark of the beast with honor and you will justify your sin with the belief in hate and false hope."

"Are saying that Joshua is a false prophet?" Antonia could not believe what he just said.

"If you are so blind do not condemn yourself more by leading others away from God." Warren continued. "Is it worth the condemnation later?"

A few of the people walked away shaking their heads while others just excused themselves with a smirk and a sigh. Some sat and talked with him while Antonia helped pick up her camera to get her tape to the studio.

"As you saw." Wilson brought back his audience. "this man, Warren, accused Joshua to being a false prophet. More on this later tonight on the eleven o'clock news."

Wilson's lights dim as he was anxious to see how it all would work out. He thought it would great.

****

Grace lay quietly in her cell wondering what could happen next. It was midnight when three inmates entered her cell which one of the guards left open. There was only a muffled scream before complete silence. Holcroft found Grace dead in the morning and ordered her to the morgue.

Word of her death came to Warren within hours and he left for the camp immediately. The news media followed him with seven news stations ready to see what would happen.

"Good evening, ladies and gentlemen, we are in front of Camp Three's mortuary where one Grace Leah was killed by a few inmates." Antonia Wilkins waited with the others to find out what would happen when Warren showed up as he promised.

After a short wait, Warren walked, seemingly without anyone noticing, through the front gate and into the morgue.

"We expect to see a very dejected man come out and probably a very upset one at that." Antonia tried to fill out empty air time. "We know little of Grace Leah other than she aided a sniper from the Patriots of Christ to kill Joshua. Wait a minute!"

Antonia saw a man running from the building. The fear on his face shocked al of them.

"Someone else is coming out…." Antonia gasped not expecting to see this new sight. "Oh, my! …. Get those cameras over to the doorway!"

Antonia was lost for words for a few seconds as Grace walked out of the morgue arm in arm with Warren.

"Ladies and gentlemen…" She hesitated. "I don't know what to say to you, but the woman who is walking out with him is Grace Leah who supposedly died. Either this is an unbelievable hoax or we just witnessed a miracle!"

The cameras rolled as Warren and Grace walked together down the stairs and onto the sidewalk toward the front gate. No one stopped them as they went.

"Ladies and gentlemen!" Antonia was almost breathless both from fascination and amazement. "This has to be a hoax because things like this just don't happen. What surprises me more is that no one is trying to stop them. Everyone is stunned, including me."

A medical doctor walked out the morgue watching Warren and Grace disappear around a corner.

"What happened in there?" Antonia shoved a microphone into his face. "Is it a hoax?"

"You tell me." The doctor was flummoxed. "She was dead and I'll swear to it."

"How are you sure she was dead?" Antonia asked him again.

"That man walked in and told me I was wrong, that she only sleeping." The doctor was still in shock. "I thought he was playing a poor joke. He walked up to her body and told her to get up. And she did!"

"How is that possible?" Antonia felt the goosebumps travel up her arm.

"You could have knocked me over with a feather." The doctor continued. "She opened her eyes and smiled at me as she stood up. Listen, I have to get away from this place."

The doctor moved away towards his car. Reporters tried to stop him, but he pulled away from them. By the time anyone thought to follow Warren and Grace, they were long gone.

****

Joshua got the news in his suite which prompted him to make hasty phone calls. Corbin put together a news conference in the downstairs lobby at the Hilton. Within minutes, thirty reporters were ready for his statement.

"I have prepared my answer to this rumor about someone being raised from the dead." Joshua shook his head with a smile. "I will ask you not to question me until I find out what has really happened."

The reporters murmured to themselves, but decided jus to listen.

"This is more of an explanation than a speech." Joshua hastily jotted down a few things when he came down in the elevator. "This is an official statement from the Foundation concerning this unique matter. We, of the Foundation, find it plausible that this girl was in a coma and awakened by this man, Warren. If she were dead, remember even Satan can raise the dead to serve his own purposes."

Again there was murmuring even some laughter from the group listening to him.

"There are reports spreading that this man, Warren...."

Joshua smiled to himself. "How many angels or messiahs can you name Warren?"

The reporters laughed and started to relax. Joshua realized he had their complete attention.

"This nonsense that Warren has been seen in more than one place at a given time is ridiculous." Joshua waved off that story. "If it were necessary, I could make you believe I was in many places at once."

Joshua looked at his audience and believed he was able to convince them it was a hoax.

"I think the possibility of a major hoax is more of an immediate answer." Joshua shrugged. "How many of you believe it?"

Most of them shook their heads and stopped taking notes.

"This man is just looking for a quick road to fame." Joshua sighed impatiently. "If it were true, my only answer would be Satan is alive and well. Many of you are members of the Foundation and know that something like this can quickly spread as a plague. Following this man will lead to madness and bring eternal damnation."

Joshua allowed a pause so that it might sink in what was the real problem.

"You must pray for the knowledge that is true." Joshua thought for a moment. "We want to see the power of God, but not the fallacy of false gods or messiahs. Now ladies and gentlemen….."

Joshua walked back to the elevator without hearing any protest from the reporters. What they didn't see was that Joshua was visibly disturbed by this unexpected event. The night is dark and quiet.

Chapter Eight

Twenty-five members of the Preservation of Jesus met inside the New Episcopalian Church of Life for an evening of fellowship in Vineland, New Jersey. The doors were purposely locked as they sang hymns and read scripture. Glenn Antler acted as their speaker for the evening. He was one of the younger members at twenty-six being a certified teacher and minister. His claim to fame was leaving the Foundation for the Son of Man to proclaim the real message of Christ. He was wanted by the Foundation for exposing the hypocrisy of Joshua.

"I want you all to remember that if we're found here that we may end up dead." Glenn warned them all. "The Foundation has put up rewards for those of us who defy the Foundation. We may or may not have a special visitor with us tonight."

The group guessed among themselves who it might be. Looking around, they did see anyone they did not know.

"The word has been passed around that this man Warren is a prophet and may come to us." Glenn was anxiously hoping it would be true. "If anyone does not want to run the risk of being caught with two individuals outside the law, feel free to leave."

No one left the room, but they were restless as they waited for their guest. After two hours there was a knock on the door that jarred all of them. Glenn looked through a crack in the door before opening it.

"It's safe, I'm alone." Warren assured him.

Glenn unbolted the door and let Warren inside. He escorted Warren to the front of the room.

"Tell us who you are?" one of the members asked before Warren even sat down.

"I have been sent to open the path." Warren answered as he sat down in front of them.

"Help us understand why you're here." Glenn settled down in his seat again. "We know you are not the Christ come again since the Second Coming will happen in the twinkling of an eye."

"I am here to fulfill a prophesy which you all will never see because if you do, there is little hope for you." Warren saw he wasn't making sense to them. "Why wonder about me when so much is happening that you should be prepared for?"

"Did you raise Grace Leah from the dead?" Glenn wanted to know first.

"She was asleep and I helped her to awaken." Warren thought it was not necessary to put himself on a higher level.

"So she wasn't dead?" Glenn was disappointed.

"Why worry about such things?" Warren wanted to get to the point of his visit.

"Why are you here then?" A young woman in the back of the room wanted to know.

"The words you were given from the beginning have been passed on through your fathers and father's fathers." Warren began to explain. "Philosophers debated God's existence and their findings were wrong. Politicians ignored the church and then overwhelmed it with people like Joshua."

"So you agree Joshua is evil." The young woman answered.

"You know the answer to that already." Warren was patient. Artists tried to paint universal truths into a god of existentialism. Writers tried to initiate universal understanding of Nature being the beginning and end of the universe. Many thought love was the only answer to bring peace to the world. The Word has given you all that you need to know and how to live. The Word gives you hope after death, but only through the Son."

"We know this already." Glenn spoke for the group.

"But you have not been tested." Warren warned them. "In this very room is a Judas among you."

They all looked at each other wondering who the Judas could be. Warren showed no signs at the one he knew was a traitor

I will leave you tonight and you will be tested. Before I go, let us pray: Our Father who is in Heaven…" Warren heard them all joining in.

"Hallowed be Your name." Each bowed and closed their eyes with some holding hands.

"Your kingdom come, Your will be done." Each of them felt a presence encompassing everyone in the room.

"On earth as it is in heaven." Glenn had tears flowing down his cheeks.

"Give us this day our daily bread." A sense of great relief was lifted from their shoulders.

"Forgive us our debts as we forgive our debtors." Many of the group felt faint.

"Lead us not into temptation, but deliver us from evil." They all were one in prayer now. "For yours is the Kingdom, the Power and the Glory, Amen."

As they all looked up. Warren was gone. No one heard him leave. Glenn told them to all go home and be vigilant.

****

"Good morning, ladies and gentlemen." Antonia Wilkins stood in front of the building Glenn and his followers had met Warren. "It was reported that here in this, the New Episcopalian Church of Life building, the man called Warren met with the Preservation of Jesus. Here he denounced Joshua as well as mocked the great artists and writers of our time. He spoke of the end times...."

Antonia abruptly stopped her commentary as she saw Warren speaking with a little boy and his mother.

"We can find out ourselves as he is not twenty feet away from us." Antonia was pleased to have an exclusive.

Warren turned to confront her waiting for whatever questions she might ask.

"Our viewers would like to know if believe you are a prophet of God?" Antonia shoved her mike under Warren's nose.

"What do you say?" Warren was bemused by the question.

"I saw you are a great con man trying to deceive everyone." Antonia honestly answered him.

"If deception was the answer, then all of you would be following me." Warren easily answered her.

"At one point in another venue you talked about one staying and another leaving." Antonia looked at her notes. "What is that all about?"

"How can you understand the concept if you have never read it?" Warren was purposely cryptic.

"Where is Grace?" Antonia changed the subject. "You supposedly raised her from the dead? Everyone thought she was dead, but evidently not. Was it a hoax?"

"She's not dead." Warren refused to fully answer. "You are the ones who say she was dead."

"You warn everyone that God is alive and will judge all of us." Antonia tried to get a straight answer from him. "Some people do not believe God exists. What do you say about that?"

"God is a rock that is always there where you pass away." Warren saw the confused face on Antonia. "You will pass away, but God, a rock will always be here. How can you deny the existence of something that is always here? Grace came to me and like moss clung to me. You walk by, pick me up and throw me out of your path."

"There ladies and gentlemen." Antonia turned to her camera visibly upset. "You have heard for yourselves, that this man has a direct connection to God. I now return you to our studio for the day's news."

The cameras shut down and Antonia knew they were off camera when she approached Warren who was walking away.

"Hey Jesus! Calvary is the other way!" Antonia believed he was crazy. She felt better as she entered her van with the crew to go back to the studio.

****

"John." Joshua interrupted him Corbin who is reading over one of his sermons for a future service. "We are the most fortunate people of this earth. Here we are planning to set this man Warren up for his own destruction and he's doing most of the work himself."

"And it's being reported to millions of people." Corbin agreed. "But I'm worried about his getting more followers that could cause us trouble."

"We'll make him out to be such a fanatic, they won't follow too long." Joshua brushed off the possibility. "He demands nothing for their loyalty except himself. He speaks nonsense about everlasting life which the media will eat up. We have the corner marketing salvation and most of the world is very comfortable with our ideas."

A knock on the door breaks into their conversation. Joshua gestures to John to answer it.

"Excuse me, sir." One of Joshua's aides excused himself. "There are a number of reporters who would like an interview with Joshua."

"Of course." Joshua answered for himself. "I'll be right down."

Corbin closed the door and wondered what Joshua would have to say to the reporters at this time.

"I'd rather you stayed here until after my interview." Joshua picked up his jacket and began to walk toward the door. "I won't be long because I'll just say a few things to water their mouths. Maybe let them wonder what I could have said. See you later."

Joshua left for the elevator and entered the room full of reporters and cameras. A podium was hastily made so that he could see them all.

"What are your thoughts about this man Warren?" The first question was asked just as he turned toward them.

"I have been asked this question a number of times." Joshua smiled expecting the question. "I think this man is disturbed and a dangerous con man who is trying to destroy the Foundation of the Son of Man. He plans to destroy this country with his egotism. He impresses me more as an Anti-Christ figure than a Christ figure."

"What are your plans as to keeping him from disrupting the nation?" The next question was expected.

"I plan to speak against him and allow public opinion decide what should be done with him." Joshua deftly side stepped the question.

Would you condone whatever measures necessary to quiet him?" A reporter from the back called out.

"I will not condone violence unless it was an act of God." Joshua tried to measure his words. "I have no choice, but let God and you gentlemen bring out the truth."

"We have been told that this man has condemned you and what you represent." The first reporter asked. "Although he hasn't said so, Warren implied that you are the Anti-Christ."

"This only proves my point that this man is deranged."

Joshua bristled slightly at the accusation. "He is jealous of my position in the Foundation."

Joshua was happy that he was given an opportunity to push the blame to Warren and hoped strengthened his position.

"He finds it gratifying to try and destroy what he cannot himself attain." Joshua continued his attack. Gentlemen, this insanity must be ignored and is worth the waste of time it really is. I just hope no one gets hurt from his rantings."

Joshua held up one finger to let them all know that he would entertain only one more question.

"Is it possible that the Foundation can do anything to help this man?" A reporter from the back of the room asked. "It is evident he needs spiritual direction. Are you prepared to confront him and bring him back to the fold?"

Miracles are performed when someone is beyond hope." Joshua knew what the reporter meant. "It is not a means to win the battle of minds. I don't think God would want someone to be changed if it a means to be a part of history. Wouldn't it be great if this man is here to fulfill the prophesy of the coming of an anti-Christ? The Foundation will be here always to help anyone who is in fear of this man. Now, I'm sorry gentlemen, I have affairs to take care of for the Foundation."

There were cries of "Wait a minute!" "Just one more question!" and Could you clarify!", but Joshua never looked back as he returned to the sanctuary of the elevator and his room.

Chapter Nine

The phone rings in Joshua's suite where is having breakfast. Impatiently he looked for Corbin, but decided he would have to answer it himself.

"Hello… Oh, hello Michael!" Joshua greeted Michael who was part of his eyes and ears. He shifted to his chair overlooking the city when Corbin came into the room patiently waiting for Joshua to finish.

"Yes, I understand." Joshua lowered his voice. "And you know what to do with them?… Okay then, call back when you're finished."

"What's up, Joshua?" Corbin saw the concerned look on Joshua's face.

"Michael suspected a few of the Preservation of Jesus had met in Vineland, New Jersey." Joshua thought for a second.

"What's wrong?" Corbin saw trouble.

"They met with Warren and there could trouble from them." Joshua answered.

"I worry about the Preservation because they are the largest group that have been fighting us." Corbin paced the floor.

"I'm forced to let Michael readjust their thinking." Joshua stared out the window.

"We are trying to save everyone with the Foundation and there is so much opposition." Corbin could not understand why something had to be done.

"Well, you never know who wants to get us after we made it clear to the right path to God." Joshua randomly told Corbin what he already knew. "Our way is the only way to peace."

Joshua sat and stared out the window and was quiet. Corbin knew that their conversation was over.

****

Glenn Antler addressed thirty-five members about the future of the Preservation of Jesus. Each member was warned about the danger of their presence at the Vineland Church speaking about it.

"We will find ourselves unable to contend physically with the Foundation or the Patriots of Christ, but we need to be spiritually fit to overcome the pain, both physical or mental, that is to come to us soon." Glenn was concerned that the Foundation had already about this meeting."

Some of the group shifted nervously even though no one left the building.

"We are to be strong we feel weak." Glenn continued. "We must be able to laugh when we want to cry…"

Glenn was interrupted by the sound of motorcycles outside the church. Within minutes the lights went out. A look out the window, Glenn saw fifteen bikers walking towards the building.

"What should we do?" One of the group asked.

Glenn saw the bikers with chains and knives coming close. Some of the members escaped to their vans and sped away. The bikers broke down the door and started to beat anyone who stayed behind. Glenn was knocked unconscious as the bikers started a fire leaving those inside to fight the flames and save themselves.

Some of the bikers followed the vans and tried to force them off the roads. One of the bikers and a van collided crashing into a ditch which killed all those involved. Three bikers picked up their dead comrade and rode away.

People in nearby houses came out and called the fire department to save the church. Glenn is pulled out to await an ambulance. The bikers were long gone when help finally arrived. The church was not saved.

****

"We interrupt this program to bring you a special report from Vineland, New Jersey." Andrea Wilson interrupted a variety of programs with her special report. "Just hours ago, at this Vineland, New Jersey church, members of the Preservation of Jesus were attacked and the church burned to the ground. Just down the road a van carrying three members of the church crashed in a ditch just one mile from this point."

The camera panned down the road without a view of

the crushed vehicle. Andrea was less than enthusiastic about the assignment.

"Police suspect an illegal gathering of the Preservation of Jesus caused a confrontation with bikers passing by." Andrea looked as tired as she was. "Here is Captain Johnson of the Vineland Police Department who has more information for us."

"Yes, the members of the Preservation all were not wearing the armbands of the Foundation and were illegal congregating without permission." Johnson was irritated to have his town become a notorious news item. "We have a witness that they were planning events against the Foundation."

"Thank you, Captain Johnson." Andrea walked away and stood confronting the camera. "The Preservation of Jesus are known to ask members to ignore the use of armbands and therefore defy the Foundation. President Avery has spoken out that this demonstration against the government and the Foundation will not be tolerated."

"Turn off the news, John." Joshua heard enough.

"This killing wasn't necessary." Corbin was disturbed that Joshua would condone this violence. "You have to control Michael or we will find ourselves involved in this mess."

"Those who refuse to wear the armbands and illegally plot against us must be challenged." Joshua rationalized the sad actions. "They must learn the wrath of God awaits those who disobey his actions. God will not stand for insults against Him and His decrees. "I'm sorry John, but it was justified. We can't be held accountable if they won't listen."

"I don't disagree with you except that it isn't necessary to kill those who oppose us." Corbin wondered if he heard right. Has Joshua become the sole authority of the events that were to come? "We need the comparison of our cause to their churches that offer nothing but rhetoric."

"I know, but we can't have them get to dangerous with a correction." Joshua wondered if Corbin was up to the task. "Too much rope and…."

The cell phone range with the tune "March of the Wooden Soldiers" on Joshua line.

"Yes, Michael!" Joshua was pleased to hear from him. "I'm pleased to a certain extent that you broke things up…" Joshua waited as Michael explained himself. "But we cannot have too much killing. We wanted to a point that the survivors could share. Dead bodies cannot share anything... Fine, I understand this time.... God bless you, too. Good-bye."

Corbin looked at Joshua and shook his head unconvinced this was the right path to take. He had joined the Foundation long ago and it had changed so much over the past two years.

"Feel better now?" Joshua turned his attention to a stack of papers on his desk. He was content to have the news in the background even though he hardly listened to any of it.

****

Glenn Antler's head hurt while what was left of his friends surrounded him with concerned looks. They had been praying for his recovery and wondered what they would do if Glenn had died.

"We're frightened." A young woman confessed.

"I know, I know." Glenn reached out to her and held

her hand. "We can't let them keep us from the path made for us."

"We'd better get home before we're caught, too." Another started toward the door. "It seems to be over."

"Keep in touch." Glenn asked them. He knew some of them would not come back because of family concerns.

****

The newspapers have the whole story." Corbin burst into the room. "One of the Preservation confessed that the organization was going to strike against the Foundation. This story made front page news throughout the country. I think our sanctions will if the threat of violence is on the table."

"Don't count on it." Joshua tried to calm Corbin down. "We don't have to be concerned about Warren. Even if some take him seriously we can convince the right people to stay with us."

"All mad men have mad men as followers." Corbin interjected with a smile.

"Yes, and some of them carry guns." Joshua reminded Corbin. "We need more conferences before Monday. "We need a great crowd for the Times Square gathering. I want to insure Warren's downfall just before I speak."

"The Foundation's finest hour is coming and I thank God that I'm part of it!" Corbin was overjoyed while Joshua shook his head. "Everything we've worked for is coming to fruition."

"Take it easy, John." Joshua cautioned with a smile. "You're talking to me remember. It's all evident."

"Sorry." Corbin was chastised and sat down. "I'm just excited about how far with gotten to make history."

"Well, right now we have a breakfast engagement with Judge Conroe and our friends." Joshua stood up to go. "So, let's go."

Joshua and Corbin, escorted by six security guards, walked to the Greek Isle Restaurant where others were waiting with Judge Conroe. Joshua always had his guests waiting so he could enter last with all eyes on him.

"Joshua, John, glad you could make it." Conroe never knew if Joshua would show up. They shook hands extending cordialities before sitting down to eat.

"Joshua, I'm afraid we have huge problems developing." Conroe immediately brought up the reason he was there. "More and more people are removing their armbands with some burning them in protest. They deny the Foundation and favor this man Warren who speaks more for them than himself. The courts are overloaded with cases against the Foundation."

"It was expected to happen." Corbin answered for Joshua.

"Things were going so well, now this Warren shows up and it's beginning to snowball against us." Irving Greene. A lower court judge was just as concerned. "We spent too many years getting this far to have one man, insane or not, bring trouble to our cause."

"You're jumping to conclusions too fast." Joshua ordered a Greek salad.

"All of you must remember that in situations where people aren't sure of themselves." Corbin addressed the judges. "They try both sides of an issue and I think these [people only a few who will turn forever from the Foundation. You have to expect things like this with so many ignorant people that grasp onto anything that is different. We will offer an olive branch to those who have been imprisoned for political reasons that if show their allegiance to the state and Foundation all will be forgiven."

"The Foundation will do it can to bring back to the fold, but if they continue to rebel God will have his way." Joshua interjected between bites. "Everyone must separate themselves from the Patriots of Christ, the Preservation and this man Warren."

"It may get worse with the deaths within this group in New Jersey." Conroe was still concerned.

"It'll only get worse if we give this man, Warren, too much attention." Corbin tried to pass off Warren's importance.

"All right, we'll stay on the course before this becomes a crisis." Greene was not convinced, but was willing to wait.

"Remember history, gentlemen." Joshua order his main meal and turned to his guests. "They will claim they are being persecuted as the early Christians were, but it will fall on deaf ears. We offer so much monetarily, work, business and politically. Who can defeat us?"

The waiter came back and took more orders in a restaurant that was empty except for Joshua and his friends. They discussed mundane politics and points of law. When they finished, the waiter returned and motioned to Joshua.

"There's a man who wants to see you in the kitchen." The waiter whispered to Joshua.

"Who is he?" Joshua stood up to follow him. He waved away security as he left the room.

"I don't know." The waiter shrugged. "He just said he's a friend with information, but if you needed a name, he said Karl."

Joshua puzzled with the name until he entered the kitchen. He was face to face with Karl one of the Patriots assassins. Joshua noticed he wore the armband of the Foundation which allowed Joshua to relax.

"My name is Karl." He looked behind Joshua. "I was supposed to do a job for you and then be helped out of the country. I was told you could help me."

"What are you talking about?" Joshua asked fully realizing who Karl was and knowing one of them would not get out of the kitchen alive.

"You know." Karl did not like playing cat and mouse. "Michael told me it was you who set things up."

The waiter was a few feet away leaning towards the knives and chopping tools.

"If you can get me out, Michael will give you documents that will useful against Warren." Karl looked into Joshua's eyes and saw a certain deadness behind them.

"If you have documents that is of use to us, show me," Joshua reached out knowing that there were no documents to be had.

"They're right here." Karl reached into his inside pocket and started to bring out a gun. Before he brings it out the waiter behind him shoved a knife into his back. Karl turned and shot the waiter. Both fell dead.

Chaos broke out as the rest of Joshua's party either left the room or his guards came rushing in. They were too late as two bodies bled out on the floor. Joshua calmly left the kitchen and faced Corbin.

"I want to have a meeting with this Warren." Joshua slightly gritted his teeth. "I want to have it as soon as you find out where he is. I want reporters there to cover every word and every action taken. Do it now."

"Alright Josh." Corbin looked over Joshua's shoulder. "You sure you're all right?"

"Perfectly." Joshua looked around. "I guess our meeting is over."

"They ran when they heard the shot." Corbin sneered. "Do you think it's wise to call him out into the open? Wouldn't that give the impression we're taking him seriously?"

"Why worry?" Joshua shook his head thinking Corbin should be aware of everything he planned to do. "Are you not fed? Do you not have a roof over your head? Just stand with me."

Corbin turned and left as Joshua sat back down and finished his meal while the two bodies were taken out the back of the restaurant.

****

"Ladies and gentlemen." Andrea Wilson again was center stage speaking into the monitor. "It is hard for this reporter to understand all the events that have happened ever since this man Warren has come into the news. In two weeks it is if chaos has reigned around the Foundation of the Son of Man and a man called Warren."

Andrea paused for a second and moved to the right of the studio. She lifted her eyes as if peering into the audience before her.

"Joshua was almost killed today by an assassin named only as Karl, but the quick thinking of a waiter inside the Greek Restaurant saved his life." Andrea added a little emotion to her story. "Jerry Atkinson gave his life to save the leader of the Foundation. Questions remain who this man Karl worked for. Was a friend of this man, Warren, who has come out of nowhere to oppose the Foundation itself?"

Andrea stepped over to a map of the city and pointed to areas where Warren had been seen.

"We asked people in these areas of the city what they think of Warren." Andrea stood in front of the map. "What can we expect of a meeting that Joshua is calling for and find out who this man think he is? Many people have been seen talking with Warren and we wonder how quickly he has been able to be seen so many places in so short a time."

Andrea placed her hands in front of her as she continued to speak to her audience.

"A warning has been given by President Avery that he wants everyone who supports this country and the Foundation to wear their armbands." Andrea tried to give the intonation of concern as she spoke. "This could be a horrendous hoax brought by the Patriots of Christ to confuse and divide our society. Joshua expects to expose Warren for what is and that is a professional con man. Stay tuned and we will bring you up to date on the evening news."

****

Warren walked the streets of New York with Grace Leah while reporters struggled to follow them. Spectators recognized who he was and began to mill around them both.

"What are you doing here?" A reporter stuck a microphone from Warren to Grace.

"Do you realize that you are causing trouble?" A bystander yelled out at Warren.

"Millions of people want you to let them know if you

believe you have supernatural powers." Another reporter shouted out.

Grace laughed at the question, but strayed on the side of Warren who just kept walking.

"I represent National News Television and we heard that you brought this woman back from the dead." Eva Bastion stood in front of them both. "Is it true or not?"

"Many of you here and those listening to my voice know what is true and what isn't." Warren stopped as he found himself surrounded by the crowd.

"God is not a fantasy molded by the imagination of those who have corrupted the church." Grace refused to keep silent. "He is not an heirloom passed on to family members from generation to generation. You tolerate His presence until it's time to decide whether you are with him or against Him."

"Empty words offered up hoping that you can bargain with God and Joshua will not do." Warren offered to those who were listening. "You follow a false prophet that will lead you to complete destruction and you do because it brings you comfort. Jesus said to pick up the Cross and follow me. How many of you dare to do such a thing?"

"What cross? Are you saying Joshua is a false prophet?" Eva was almost at a loss for words.

"This is what I say for the Lord, that if you have seen My face, I will never leave you." Grace answered.

"Your face?" Eva could not understand.

"A tree is used for shade, for comfort and for construction." Warren realized nothing they said would make sense to them. "If you need shelter, you cut down the tree and build a house. When the storm comes, you have a safe haven. Those who are cut down for the Lord's sake will help build a home in heaven."

"We know scripture, too." Eva was not impressed. "Do you agree that we are to be like little children…to act and think like them. If we did, how could we live in this terrible time of war and distrust?"

"It was never meant to act like children, but be subservient to God as children." Warren was impatient. "Learn as children what God has to offer you and know that He is control in the worst of times."

"Do you believe in the Preservation of Jesus?" Eva asked random questions hoping for a sound bite.

"I believe in the Son of God, Jesus the Christ." Warren faced the crowd who was becoming nervous. "Neither the

Patriots of Christ nor the Preservation of Jesus will change the Foundation of the Son of Man."

"We talked with both of them that violence is not the answer." Grace stared through Eva.

"What is the answer?" Eva thought she could get her sound bite.

"No one person can tell you that He is here or He is there for when Jesus comes again it will be in a twinkling of an eye." Warren tried to continue down the street. "Be wary. Be ready."

"What about Grace you supposedly brought back to life?" Eva followed them.

"You have eyes, but you cannot see the truth that is right in front of you." Warren kept a head of her.

"That's not an answer." Eva was frustrated. "I don't know that it's true."

"Then find the truth." Grace looked back at her. "Don't let others what is true."

"Are you part of this hoax?" Eva tried to get a rise out of either of them.

"The only hoax comes from the Foundation who fears the truth. If you are so concerned go to your leaders and ask them what they believe in."

Here the crowd started to move around making a path for Grace and Warren to move ahead. Another part of the gathering moved out of the way of a limo carrying Joshua and Corbin that stopped next to Warren. Loud murmuring brought up the excitement of the meeting of the two talked about individuals in the world.

"We meet again, but I cannot accept you as an equal." Joshua refused to offer his hand. He didn't want to take the chance Warren would not take it.

"We are not equals so I am surprised you are here." Warren showed no emotion.

"I was passing by and saw the crowds then I saw you." Joshua offered.

"Are you so concerned that I will threaten your power?" Warren knew why Joshua was there. "You can control some minds, but they are weak. Your time is very short."

"You don't make sense to me or those around us." Joshua stepped closer trying to intimidate Warren. "I am the authority of the Foundation and am a counselor to the President of the United States. I confer with the Pope and most of Europe. China and Russia. What can you say you have done?"

"You are your own authority." Warren was not impressed. "The Foundation will soon fall and you have no say. You speak for yourself not for God."

"Who are you top judge him?" Corbin was irate. "The Foundation has saved millions from famine, violence and poverty."

"None will see the kingdom of Heaven." Warren calmly waved his hand at Corbin who found himself unable to speak. "You do things in your name and it means nothing to the Lord you think you worship."

"You dare confront me with that?" Joshua sounded irritated. "You refuse to speak with anyone who opposes you except with veiled threats. I implore you people to wash your hands of this charlatan. If you follow him, you will condemn yourselves with the Foundation, but, also, God Almighty!"

"Careful how you call upon God." Warren spoke softly to Joshua. "He may answer you with a lightning bolt."

"This is idiotic." Joshua pushed his way back to his limo and almost left Corbin behind. Warren and Grace went their way, too.

Reporters soon gave up on following them when they stopped to talk with the homeless and the prostitutes. Warren sat with sick alcoholics while Grace walked down the street on her own.

Chapter Ten

"All you hear outside and in the media is talk, talk, talk, but nothing is done!" Paul Houltz shouted as the leader of the Patriots of Christ. Houltz is thirty-four and the active mouthpiece of an organization that was known for its violence. He was already a balding man with scars from confrontations with the Foundation and the Preservation of Jesus.

"Peace, God, love and Jesus as our revolutionary leader would not have sat idly by while two fact ions try His patience." Houltz continued. "Talking will not get us anywhere, but doing well."

The gathering crowd that gathered for his speech yelled its approval to Houltz. Reporters in the back of the crowd jotted down what they thought they heard than what was said.

"If they try and destroy us, we must protect ourselves!" Houltz continued waving his hands and slapping the podium. "I know we are being persecuted and Jesus would not have us sit by and be slaughtered. It is close to Armageddon and we will be at the forefront of Christ's army that will destroy the powers of Satan that surround us!"

As the crowds roared approval, Houltz raised his hands in victory. He left the podium to direct a demonstration through the streets against the Foundation. He raises an American flag and begins to lead them away.

****

Glenn Antler and fifteen other members of the Preservation of Jesus met with Grace and Warren in Nyack, New York. From there they traveled to Hook Mountain where listening devices were scarce. Warren takes them near the top of the mountain overlooking the Hudson River.

"I've brought you here…" Warren stopped abruptly seeing John Wise in the group. "Have you come to kill me, John?"

John was at loss for words since he tried to add a false beard and a scar to hide his identity. He froze as Warren came and embraced him.

"Join us and if you are convinced not to walk with me." Warren smiled as John struggled with his conscious. "I will allow you to shoot me."

"All right." Was all John could say.

"I've brought you here to speak of things you need to know before the time to come." Warren nudged Grace to stand next to John. "You are not the only ones hearing the voice of Christ at this time. Many small groups are being visited to be prepared for the future. You've lost some of your friends yet your faith is strong. I am here to tell you that violence is not the answer though you will be persecuted."

Grace took out a large purse and brought to Warren a small bottle of wine and half a loaf of bread. Warren picked at the bread and poured small cups of wine having Grace pass them out.

"As Jesus said "This is my body broken for you." Warren gave each one wine and bread. "Take eat. Take drink for Jesus said "This is my blood was shed for you". Truly you are His disciples and will have many trials yet to come."

The group was amazed that from such a small bottle of

wine that everyone was served and the half loaf of bread fed them all.

"It is time to go and speak to those who are servants of the Foundation." Warren got up with Grace and started down the mountain.

"Is there anything else?" Glenn thought it was such a long journey for so short a time together. "Where do you go next?"

"There is a traitor within your group." Warren put his arm around Glenn. "Anything I say will go right to Joshua. Be careful."

"Who is it?" Glenn did not get an answer. Instead Warren and Grace continued through the trail and just past a turn Glenn saw they were gone.

****

"One thing you must realize." Joshua spoke to a large gathering in Central Park. Tens of cameras and hundreds of reporters took down his every word. "This man Warren that you insist we talk about is a fraud, hypocrite to all that the Foundation stands for, deceitful, a dangerous demagogue. We, of the Foundation of the Son of Man, want you to know our position that God is on our side. We want you to stay in the fold so that no one will be condemned unless you stray from the path. Those who have strayed come back be forgiven."

Joshua tried to look as many in the eye as he could. Corbin raised his arms to the sky giving the impression he was calling upon God for help.

"It is vitally important to all of us that you acknowledge your loyalty and dedication to the Foundation." Joshua held up a card. "Sign these cards and receive the blessing of those who look after you. This is the age of anti-Christ and he is here amongst you. The ushers will pass these out as the service progresses. It might be good to know that President Avery has signed one of these cards. Even he is under the protection of the Foundation. Let us bow our heads for a few moments in prayer."

Everyone bowed their heads as they took cards from Joshua's ushers. There was a short silence before a great choir sang "Lord, Take These Burdens From Me." When the choir finished Joshua again addressed the throng of people.

"I am happy to see so many of you here this afternoon." Joshua smiled broadly. "I had hoped and prayed for such a gathering to hear the words God has given to me to say to you. This is the time when God is looking for those who will take the chance to do His bidding even though a false prophet calls you away. We, the Foundation of the Son of Man, must undertake the most important step anyone has ever taken before. We must determine what new direction the Foundation must go as someone who some perceive as a Prophet. This man brings violence and confusion which we must address as a nation."

Joshua looked to Corbin who nodded his approval though Joshua didn't need it. A look of pride shone through the gathering as Joshua raised his arms as if to embrace all of them.

"We want to tear away the walls that keep us from joining hands and walking together in peace and love." Joshua now was full of a spirit he didn't recognize. "I want you to know that I am the true prophet that God has ordained to lead you forward. It is not out of ego I tell you this, but humble fact."

Many of those attending started to murmur about

what they just heard. Some applauded thought they didn't understand what was just said.

"This is a time that you know the truth and the symbol of that truth to keep you safe." Joshua ignored the murmuring. "This is a trying time for the Foundation and it is necessary to be blunt about the foolishness you are hearing. This man called Warren is dangerous. Why would God send a prophet named Warren? It is ridiculous that he has the ability to save anyone. He quotes scripture, but the devil can quote scripture and expect you to follow him."

Joshua felt a twinge within his soul that strengthened him as he spoke. He was already off the message he planned to use, but it didn't matter now.

"Think hard before you follow him." Joshua paced back and forth on the stage. "Remember those who depend on your faith. Think of what you will lose and what you will do to the Foundation that you follow. The dangers that you will face you can never imagine. I want you to remember my words when you realize the truth that many charlatans will come to you. Now before we disband, our choir will sing for you."

The choir stood up and sang "Remember us." Joshua

turned to Corbin who had a look of concern on his face.

"What?" Joshua asked him.

"That was too close." Corbin wondered what Joshua was thinking.

"What was?" Joshua did not understand.

"You told them that you were the true prophet." Corbin saw that Joshua did not understand. "You let everyone know that you one step from God Himself."

"Maybe it's time for someone to lead them." Joshua moved passed Corbin toward his waiting limo. "Would you mind giving the benediction?"

****

"Good evening ladies and gentlemen. This is Jim Hansen here with the news." Hansen shuffled the papers in front of him which were really blank since he used a teleprompter. "The big news tonight is that of three major organizations of the country, each voicing its opinion on the present outbreaks of violence and this man of the hour named Warren."

Hansen shifted in his seat as he waited for the cameras were readjusted.

"he Patriots of Christ held an earlier meeting today and discussed the possibility of demonstrating against the persecution from the Foundation of the Son of Man. At the same time the Preservation of Jesus has been reported to stand against the demands of the Foundation to make loyal citizens wear an armband to show their loyalty. All this centers around the controversy of who this Warren really is."

Hansen shuffled a few blank pages and stared back into the teleprompter.

"Joshua, leader of the Foundation, seemed worried as he spoke in Central Park just hours ago." Hansen used his good looks to full advantage as he lifted one eyebrow in wonder. "He warned his listeners that Warren was a dangerous fraud and it would lead to repercussions from the government. President Avery added to the controversy when he insisted that all citizens should for the sake of peace wear armbands to show unity."

Joshua took a deep breath before moving to the next segment of his story.

"Joshua declined that he was concerned about Warren himself." Hansen almost smiled, but constrained himself. "He wanted his followers to follow the direction of the Foundation and God who, Joshua insists is on his side. It is inferred that some people think Warren is a new prophet. Rumors of miracles have been sent around that Warren has emphasized his right to be the new prophet. We only have to wait and see how things shape up in the next few days as to how Joshua will handle the situation. In other news tonight…."

Chapter Eleven

"To you I tell that I have little patience for those who think they can have both what Joshua offers and what I bring to you." Warren addressed a large gathering in corning, New York. "It is written that 'I know your works, that you are neither hot nor cold and I would rather you were hot or cold. So then because you are lukewarm and neither hot nor cold, I will spew you out of my mouth.' Your churches fight over political correctness amongst yourselves and you leave the Lord in the background."

Warren had been quiet too long and decided to speak to those who would listen.

"It is also written that 'him that overcomes I will make a pillar in the temple of my Father." Warren continued as police started to form behind the gathering. "'and I will write upon him the name of my Father and the name of the city of my Father and I will write upon him my new name.'"

The police started to move forward as Warren raised his hand which seemed to freeze their approach.

"So I say." Warren kept his hand up high. "If economy is important to you and the hunger of others is not; if you want to be safe and not find misery standing for the Lord; and one day you shout the name of the Lord and the next shudder in fear of the Foundation; you are lukewarm and will be spewed out His mouth. Denial in these times because you expected wealth and prosperity, comfort and leisure, then your Father in heaven will deny you. Yet you will be blessed if you stand now and speak for the Lord your God. It doesn't mean you might lose your life, but it may mean entering the Kingdom of God."

The police were becoming agitated for not being able to move ahead.

"I will not force you to follow Jesus because you know the path is narrow and only the strong can follow." Warren raised his hand higher. "You will not be chosen you must volunteer. Know this though, if you follow Jesus and renounce the Foundation, you may be sacrificing your lives. You must deny yourselves and stop being spectators."

Sirens could be heard in the distance which unnerved those who shifted around Warren.

"As far as I am concerned you judge for yourselves where the truth lies." Warren smiled down at them all. "But it seems that you have lived in darkness for so long that the light is questioned."

Now Warren looked into the cameras that were focused on everything he said.

"You're set in your ways." He seemed to speak through the lens into those who were watching. "So deep are you that you are drowning in your own gluttony of countless doctrines that still divide you. You have read into the scriptures what you wanted to hear instead of practicing what was said to you. You ignore each other because one doctrine doesn't agree with another. You have read into the scriptures what you wanted to hear. Even then you do not practice what you preach. You love yourselves more than others."

The police tried to push through the crowds, but found it impossible.

"I am here for a short time only to give you the

knowledge of the Lord." Warren took a breath. "I am going to Jerusalem as I leave here."

Warren nodded to Grace who pulled John from the crowd. Warren stepped down and lowered his hand as sirens blared and the police started to make arrests. Some were attacked with clubs as they ran in all directions.

"Why don't you help us?" A man ran past Warren.

"Because it is time." Warren continued around a corner and was gone.

"Where is he?" Two officers were looking for Warren.

"He's yours." The man drooped his shoulders a little. "He has left us behind."

John and Grace hurriedly walked by both of them without being recognized.

"I know a place where we'll be safe." John took Grace's hand pulling her down the street.

"We will never be safe from this point on." Grace knew John did not understand her meaning, but followed him anyway.

"Your friend has a knack for disappearing." John was curious. "Who is he really?"

"He is a warning that things are about to change." Grace continued to be vague. "You are an instrument of death not a warrior for Christ."

"I used to believe in the cause...." John's voice trailed off. "Now it's just a job. Nothing I do changes anything."

"Then listen to me and be saved from yourself." Grace pulled away from him. "Jesus is the way, the truth and the life. Give up your weapons and soon everything will change for you."

"I used to believe that, too." John smiled somewhat condescendingly.

"Death follows you now." Grace had an odd look in her eyes which made John uncomfortable.

"Weren't you dead once." John had heard the stories about her.

"Now I am alive." Grace's eyes seemed to light up. "Let me tell you a mystery...."

They walked and she talked every so often ducking into

alleyways as patrol cars passed by. John listened, nodding as she spoke to him in whispers.

****

"Welcome ladies and gentlemen." Patricia Ohlman wasted no time to place herself in front of the cameras. "This is a television special featuring a new band brought to you by the Foundation of the Son of Man. Our station will present this musical presentation to thirty nations at the same time. Now we introduce Storm."

Onstage Diane Limbar came to the microphone and addressed the audience in Central Park. Storm was hand-picked by the Foundation to placate those who were attacked just a week before.

"Thank you." Diane acknowledged the applause and nodded to the security guards that walked in front of the stage. "The first thing we must tell you that those who were here last week during the violence are now welcome as brothers and sisters within the Foundation. Joshua has taught us to forgive our enemies and pray for them. Our first song is a conveyance of our feelings at this time. Many times we wonder how we can forgive when we would rather have revenge. There is a purpose where God shows us everything. Some of you wanted you run away and hide and the Foundation understands that."

Diane saw the crowd becoming anxious and told her she was talking too long.

The song is entitled "You Are Not Alone". Diane stepped back allowing the band to start playing. Then took the microphone and began to sing:

> "Lord, why do you tell me
> to love all my brothers?
> I have tried.
>
> I come back to you frightened.
> I was so peaceful at home.
> I was so settled.
>
> I felt cozy.
> I was alone.
> I was at peace.
>
> Sheltered from the rain.
> Sheltered from the wind.
> Keeping me clean.

> Hide me, shelter me
> in your ivory tower
> and keep me safe.
>
> You have gained all,
> I am your father,
> I am your God.
>
> Yes, I am your father,
> I am your God
> slipped in among you."

The crowd was silent not sure how to understand the song. Diane turned to her band to start another song:

> "Last night I had a dream
> and then dreamed again.
> He said come to me,
> come to me.
>
> Lead my people
> to the mountains
> and to the sea
> lead my people.
>
> Lead my people
> to the valleys

> and to the streams
> lead my people.
>
> Call out my name
> and listen to me.
> The Lord is here today.
> The Lord is here to stay."

There was a spattering of applause which made Diane smile. She decided not to follow the list of accepted songs and started on her own.

> "There's a time we'll need to pray,
> Got to find the right words to say.
> Here I am Lord, what can I do?
> Remake me whole, strong and new.
>
> Last night I had a dream,
> last night I had a dream
> and Jesus said come to me.
> People kneel and pray.
>
> Women cry out for help
> as men embrace their cries.
> No more to hide our faces
> being as children again.

Call out the name of the Lord,
forget what you've heard
and listen to the name of Jesus,
follow the name of the Lord."

Everyone cheered and applauded enthusiastically as Diane bowed and set her microphone in its stand.

"Let us pray." Diane bowed her head.

"Who gave them permission to go off message?" Joshua sat in his suite leaning to switch off the television.

"It's an independent station." Corbin was already on the phone to cut off air time. "The president of the network will not shut it down.

"You get him to see me tomorrow or he won't have a network to run!" Joshua fumed. "I want that concert shut down immediately. No excuses! Do it!"

"All right." Corbin anxiously made phone calls.

"I gave everyone positions to keep the Foundation together to keep these things from happening." Joshua paced back and forth. "How did this happen?"

"We'll do what we can." Irving Greene who was visiting to explain the situation concerning some disturbing events within the Foundation.

"Leave us." Joshua motioned to Greene. He picked up his papers and quickly left the room.

"Joshua. I think you're working too hard on this." Corbin sought to calm his friend down. "There's nothing that this lunatic can do to hurt the Foundation unless you make a big deal out of it."

"You don't realize." Joshua was irritated. "He has stirred up too many questions. The public questions our Foundation and we have to answer some embarrassing problems we never made known. We have to protect ourselves so our members do not think we are weak."

"Listen." Corbin put his hand on Joshua's shoulder only to have Joshua push it off.

"You know better." Joshua turned away from him.

"None of us want this to happen, but we cannot show doubt about this man." Corbin was not sure how to respond to Joshua.

"I don't doubt his insanity." Joshua sat down looking out over the city.

"Then why do you keep trying to reassure yourself and everyone else that he is mad." Corbin worried that Joshua was losing the message. "Don't you see we can't lose your confidence?"

"I'm sorry." Joshua tried to apologize. "I've just haven't been able to get enough sleep. So much has to be done. I have so many people who rely on me for their spiritual welfare."

"You should lie down." Corbin saw the tension in him.

"We'll talk later." Joshua got up to find his room.

Corbin removed himself to go downstairs to a waiting limo. As usual, reporters were waiting for any information about the state of the Foundation.

"Archbishop Corbin?" One reporter shoved a recorder into Corbin's face. "Can you tell us your own feelings to the growing dissension in the Foundation of the Son of Man?"

"My own feelings are that there is no dissension in the Foundation." Corbin was not ready for this, but was willing to answer what he could. "These people who follow a different Jesus than we know are afraid, afraid of the Foundation which holds the answer to life, wealth and future of the country and the world."

"What about this man Warren?" Another reporter called out.

"I am sure this man believes he sincere." Warren expected to be asked the question. Unfortunately, Satan is sincere about what he believes is true. This man does not follow the teachings of the Foundation and has questioned the very integrity of Joshua."

"So then." The reporter pressed Corbin. "You believe then that Warren is disciple of Satan and plans to destroy the Foundation?"

"You've said it." Corbin agreed. "More trouble can be expected if his followers of the Preservation of Jesus and the Patriots of Christ pursue violence instead a peaceful dialog. Why God allows this I do not know. God has his reasons so we cannot question His will. However, we will not sit idly by and let Satan have his way."

"What do you propose to do about him?" The first reporter questioned him.

"The Foundation will do everything possible to make sure this man is stopped short of violence." Corbin assured them. "Society will judge this man for his irrationality and encouragement for violence."

"There is a possibility that the Foundation may suffer with the repercussions that come if more follow Warren." A lady reporter chimed in. "If he is a fraud why does the Foundation concern itself? Some good things have been contributed to this man."

"Like what for instance?" Corbin realized that he might have said the wrong thing.

The reporter reeled off a number of things that even Corbin had not heard about.

"The most important event was the raising from the dead of Grace Leah." She stared into Corbin's eyes. "I was there and I saw the body and she was dead."

"How is that possible?" Corbin did not like the way the interview was going, but his limo door was blocked.

"Warren has given hope to those who wonder about a better life." Corbin realized he was talking to Amber Albright of the underground group, ASC. ASC stood for the American

Spiritual Community. "He has visited any and all homes that invite him. A revival has been growing that will outrival the Foundation."

"This man was supposedly seen in fifty different places." Corbin countered. "Does that give him god-like qualities over and above God himself?"

"And who is your God? Joshua?" Amber saw Corbin wince. "What has the Foundation of the Son of Man done to bring the spirit of Christ back into our society. The Foundation hides without helping the economy or stop the political turmoil throughout the world."

"I remember you now, Amber, and your viewers should know that the purpose of this interview is to attack the Foundation." Corbin tried to push past her, but failed. "The Foundation will not help those who are not members while Warren does not ask who the membership of any organization they are joined with. He will accept all. Why doesn't Joshua walk the streets and witness for the God he claims to follow?"

"You are obviously taken in by this lunatic? Corbin stood up straight and addressed everyone who could hear him. "Your point is well taken about Joshua mingling with the crowds in the city. However, because of so many issues that are all encompassing affecting the world, he needs to work on those issues. Joshua has had many mass meetings in large areas to let you know about what the Foundation is doing. On Monday Joshua will speak on a major stage about this man who has taken upon himself to challenge God and the Foundation."

"God being Joshua who has claimed to be the last Messiah." Amber made sure everyone heard her. "Is he that arrogant equating himself with God?"

"His reference to being a messiah was only to let everyone know that the Foundation will be the last resort to right this country and the world." Corbin tried to explain. "This man you support may well be the anti-Christ we all fear."

"Or maybe Joshua is the anti-Christ." Amber sounded out the disdain she had for Corbin.

"Joshua will speak the truth about this man who claims deity." Corbin was angry and it showed. "It is not only a problem for the foundation, but the peace and tranquility of society on the whole. You treat him like a messiah which will only corrupt your faith."

"Are you saying that in the interest of the Foundation

or your own interests?" Amber stood her ground as Corbin tried again to pass.

"The Foundation's interest should be yours as well." Corbin had had enough. "I am sure if you need to challenge us further, you can address our website and we will fully explain our position. Any more questions will have to wait. Now let me by."

Amber stepped aside letting Corbin, who was visibly flustered, a clear path to his limo. Amber quickly left the scene since security guards were rushing out of the Hilton toward her

Chapter Twelve

"I feel better." John sat next to Grace almost crying thinking of the long conversation he had with her. "I don't understand how the Jesus could forgive me, but what do we do now?"

"We are on the run so right now we have to keep moving." Grace looked around. "The Lord will let us know our purpose soon enough."

"What about Warren?" John watched a slight sadness cloud Grace's eyes.

"I won't see him again." Grace started to walk away.

"Why not?" John had given up any thought of following Warren. He decided that his mission was over and now he had to worry about the police and the Patriots of Christ. He felt he was a walking dead man.

"He is on his way to Jerusalem for a different mission in which I cannot follow." Grace waved him to follow.

"Jerusalem? What's in Jerusalem?" John was confused.

"The future." Grace only answered.

****

"Good evening, ladies and gentlemen and welcome to Meet The News." Steve Anchor, the main speaker for MTN and the Foundation of the Son of Man, looked perfect in front of the cameras. "Tonight, we have one of the leaders of the Patriots of Christ, Paul Hoults. Paul, we'd like to know what your viewpoint is in this seesaw battle between Joshua and Warren."

"I believe that Joshua planted this stooge to see who he can trust." Hoults stared at Anchor. "This stooge who acts sincere is doing nothing but following Joshua's orders. I'm sure he is well paid for this nonsense."

"Do you have any proof that he is being paid by Joshua?" Anchor jumped on the opening.

"How else can you explain that there hasn't been a

single attack on this man?" Hoults shifted in his seat. "No arrest since he was released from Camp Three?"

"That is something to think about." Anchor looked into the camera. "Yet, how do you explain the raising from the dead, Grace Leah? Doctors assured us that she was dead. Even though there were no signs of life, Warren walked in and walked out with her?"

"Money talks>" Hoults smiled broadly. "Those doctors would testify that their mothers were dead if they were paid enough. This chick was used to make people to believe in this moron. All this guy did was say a few words and took her hand as a cue to stand up. I tell you I was impressed with the audacity this guy had. I give him a lot of credit."

"So you consider this is a complete hoax." Anchor gave his audience a concerned look. "That it has its roots through the Foundation to show the weakness of those who do not believe?"

"Yes." Hoults sat back and folded his arms. "And I think people should reconsider who they have in power within the Foundation who aren't strong enough to rule this country."

"Are you saying that Joshua and his staff should be replaced?" Anchor acted astonished.

"Yes, I do." Hoults didn't hesitate.

"With who?" Anchor leaned forward to hear his answer.

"I am suggesting that this fraud should be brought out into the opening." Hoults began a rehearsed speech. "Let the people decide what to do. If it were up to me, I would have the Foundation correct the mistakes that are now being made. After the mistakes are corrected we need the people decide to elect a new leader for the Foundation."

"What mistakes are you talking about" Anchor leaned forward. "Just so our audience knows exactly what you are talking about."

"It is widely known that Joshua has full control of the Foundation of the son of Man and the actions by its members." Hoults tried to convince everyone that Joshua was the cause of all their troubles. "No one holds a position without tight security and background checks involving their business an church attendance."

"All businesses use this practice." Anchor interrupted. "I'm sure the government uses the same methods for safety of those who work in the foundation."

"Not with Joshua." Hoults started to wonder why the

Foundation allowed him to speak so long. "Joshua looks only for those who believe fully in his doctrine and goals. That you don't believe the same as the church is fine as long as you believe in Foundation. If this government instituted the same methods in ruling their citizens, there would be a revolution throughout the nation. The Foundation encourages this man, Warren, to continue to disrupt our nation, but for what purpose? Is Warren a puppet for Joshua?"

"I'm sure you are exaggerating the issues, but there is probably a grain of truth….." Anchor settled back in his chair.

"What do you mean exaggerate?" Hoults interrupted. "What I've said I've gotten from a good source and I won't stay here if you think you can humor me!"

Hoults stood up from his chair knocking it over as he left the studio, Anchor waited a while before he began taping another show.

****

"Who was that really" Joshua turned to Corbin. "He

looked like Hoults, but I met him before. This guy is close, but not him."

"We had a time to make this happen and Hoults refused to appear." Corbin was disappointed that Joshua saw the deception. "I thought it would be good for the Foundation and a bump in the news for you."

"I think it might work, but it will take hours before we know for sure." Joshua liked the idea.

"We'll make a statement with a hint of outrage if that is all right." Corbin saw the smile on Joshua's face.

"We'll wait then." Joshua leaned back enjoying the panorama of the city skyline.

****

"We have been told by word of mouth from a number of sources that there is going to be a major meeting of the Preservation of Jesus in Beaver Falls." Patricia Ohlman stood in Duffy Square waiting for Joshua to come to the podium. "At first it was thought of as a joke since Warren is already on his way to Jerusalem. However, the Preservation expect a large number of individuals to be there. Joshua today will hopefully explain the events that have happened in the last few days and what the future may hold. Here he is now and we'll listen to what Joshua has to say."

"First of all." Joshua kept a serious face as he addressed the crowd and media. "It is very unlikely many people will attend this meeting in Beaver Falls. Warren has left the country which should tell you about his lack of courage. Word has come to the Foundation that he is suicidal, perhaps hoping to be crucified by his enemies. His talk of a rapture should have everyone wondering about his sanity. Whatever he plans to do is now the problem of Israel."

Joshua shifted his position toward the cameras.

"Whatever he does it will show his intentions against us." Joshua looked hard into the cameras. "He is a liar who offers us nothing but a fantasy. "Do I want to see him fall? I'd rather we can convince to join the Foundation in a united front."

Joshua changed his position toward the crowd in front of him.

"If I am wrong about this man, I will be first to kiss his feet." Joshua raised his voice. "I am adverse to kissing anyone's feet, but I am sure that he is a false prophet. Do not tear him apart, but forgive him. Let us know if he comes back to this country so may met with him."

Joshua terminated the speech suddenly with a wave of his hand. He entered his limo and slumped wearily into the back seat. Corbin was at his side siting and staring at Joshua. He wondered if Joshua was still the pillar of the Foundation.

."

Chapter Thirteen

"This is an unbelievable sight in the history of this city of Beaver Falls." Andrew Wilson relayed his enthusiasm of the gathering crowds in the city square. "This event outdoes any concert or mass meeting ever held here. There seems to be, at least, one hundred thousand individuals meeting here. There are Jews, Catholics, Protestants and young unbelievers here to listen to who they call a new prophet even a new messiah. Many are singing Kum Ba Yah and Pass It On. The atmosphere is one of celebration. Warren was thought to be in Jerusalem, but apparently will be here in a few moments."

The cameras panned around the gathering, picking out many happy faces and those who were singing in groups.

"It is incredible." Wilson continued to fill in empty air. "That such a huge gathering could come together with just a few day's notice for this event is unprecedented. What is remarkable is that there are no drugs and no fighting even though some of those here are ex-felons, various beliefs and political agitators. There are no traffic jams inside or out of the city. I have never witnessed such widespread cooperation before."

Wilson stopped to catch his breath.

"There are businessmen, construction workers, laymen, longhairs, shorthairs, clergy you name it, they are here." Wilson was awed by what he was seeing. I have a feeling we may be witness to a great event. It is quieting down now so we will go to the stage where the group Storm is walking to their instruments."

Barbara Challey walks up to the microphone and the crowd recognizes her shouting their approval. Smiling to the audience as she picks up the microphone.

"Brothers and sisters, we are here to sing and we are here to preach the truth." Challey raised her hands. "The truth is that our Lord and Savior lives! His prophet is here tonight for the last day of freedom we will ever enjoy. We show our devotion with song and we have one for you tonight."

"Lead me on to rolling stones." Challey began to sing.

Lead me to the open tomb.
Peace from the valley of death,
the shadow of fear to dare
passing on the day from night.

People of the world complaining,
nations pushing out the twilight
of the everlasting Son.
Listen to me, listen to me
hear the calling of the Master."

"Okay. Brothers and sisters will you sing with us?" Challey called out to the receptive crowd as the song hauntingly echoes off the buildings. When they reach the last line, Warren comes forward to speak to them. Everyone is silent waiting to hear Warren speak to them. They had heard all the stories and needed to know the truth.

"I'm glad you were able to make it here as I asked you." Warren began to speak. "As you can see, I have not left for Jerusalem, yet. It will be my last destination. There is still time for many of you to spread the Word. That you are here tells the Lord you one of His own."

Some of the crowd start to sit down to listen.

"You sit or stand wondering about the real meaning of these times." Warren smiled down at them all. "Many sit and pray prayers without realizing the Lord is on your side. Blessed are you who have not seen yet believed. You are baptized through His words and get off your knees understanding that the narrow path awaits you. You cannot say 'Save me, save me' and expect an answer if you have not known the question."

Warren looked around as the crowd seemed to be spellbound with every word.

"A wandering man without a tongue tends not to debate nor does he ask forgiveness." Warren smiled. "The same can be said that if you keep your faith hidden the only future you have is to be thrown aside. I am not judge or counselor. I bring you this message only that Jesus is the Way, the Truth and the Life. No one comes to Father except through Him who calls you."

My name is not Warren, but I am one of the witnesses to whom you will never hear for you will be with the Father in heaven." Warren paced back forth on the stage. "Jesus brought you the bread of life and those who rule you have instead brought their heads on a silver platter."

"There are scars on the wrists of those who believe." Warren rolled up his shirt showing his scars. "I am not here to have you kneel before me. I am not the Christ, but one showing you the way to Him. Hear me New Israel! The past will disappear and the Lord's name will be etched in the skies above!"

The crowd cheered.

"Throw away the images you have seen." Warren's voice seemed to grow louder. "Hear New Israel, my words for you are the hope for those who will not listen! You must go back to your homes and tell everyone you see what you have heard today. If anyone push you away or laugh at you, leave him for he has made his choice. Anyone listens to you, tell them to follow so you can instruct them in the Spirit. You, New Israel, will go out to share your faith as the disciples of old."

Warren felt the Spirit spread across all those who were listening.

"Many of you now believe why I have come at this time." Warren raised his arms. "Our Father is pleased with all of you. You will always see the face of Christ and He will hear you when you call out His name. New Israel pray with me: 'Our Father, who art in Heaven, Hallowed be thy name,

Thy kingdom come, they will be done on earth as it is in Heaven, give us this day our daily bread and forgive us our debt as we forgive our debtors. And lead us not into temptation, but deliver us from evil, for thine is the Kingdom and the Power and the Glory forever. Amen! Amen! Amen!"

Warren left the stage walking behind a partition as Challey came back onstage.

"We'll sing 'Day From Night' one more time." Challey wiped the tears from her eyes. "Then the day's activities will be over. God bless all of you who came to celebrate Jesus."

Challey led the crowd in song as Wilson broke into the celebration interrupting the viewing of the home audience.

"I...don't...know." Wilson wiped tears from his own eyes. "How to...express the emotion... feeling here right now."

Wilson started weeping uncontrollably as the station quickly cut to the singing crowds. Some were already leaving while others milled around hugging each other.

****

"Awfully cute and quite emotional." Joshua switched off the television.

"I have to say that I thought he was in Jerusalem." Corbin couldn't understand how the information was wrong. "He was a good speaker, but nothing like you."

"He's a bumbling idiot." Joshua shocked Corbin with the sudden outburst. "He calls people to come to spend the day singing and waiting for his speech. Then he comes and leaves within ten minutes. He didn't even stay for an altar call! It wasn't even a meeting. I was disappointed since I have nothing to really attack. He'll learn soon enough that no one follows a ghost. Where did he go?"

Corbin turned to Judge Conroe who was taking in everything silently.

"What do you think?" Corbin asked him.

"I feel we made a mistake with this man." Conroe tried to be careful with his words.

"Do you think?" Corbin looked to Joshua.

"Maybe, we'll see." Joshua was already convinced.

"The real problem is that neither of you understand what's happening." Conroe stood up to leave.

"Have you changed allegiances?" Joshua stared hard at Conroe.

"No, but I understand things are changing." Conroe waited a moment before speaking. "This is our last meeting, Joshua, until this is straightened out. I hope it's not too late."

"Don't come back." Joshua waved him away,

"I feel free." Conroe felt relieved leaving Corbin open-mouthed with arms outstretched.

Chapter Fourteen

"Hundreds of thousands of followers of the Foundation of the Son of Man and the World Church have congregated to hear their prophet Joshua speak to them." Warren Long straightened his tie as he spoke. "You can feel the electricity and the excitement of the crowds in the air. "We all want to know how Joshua will try to counteract the effect of Warren who spoke at Beaver Falls. At this moment, Warren is in Jerusalem at this very moment saying he is a witness for God."

Long looked over the far end of the street hoping to see Joshua's limo come into view.

"A special security guard has been assigned to this meeting tonight." Long tried to fill air time until Joshua showed up. "Will Joshua announce that he plans to be the is world's new Messiah to counteract the claims of Warren's followers that he is the true prophet of God."

Long hesitated for a moment thinking he saw the limo, but was disappointed.

"It would bring great relief and a boost to the Foundation if Joshua would announce to be the leader or messiah to dispel the confusion." Long was getting anxious. The thought of walking up to the podium was a possibility even though the crowds were thick.

A silence enveloped the crowd as Joshua and Archbishop Corbin made their appearance to a round of applause. Corbin looked uncomfortable as Joshua held his head up high.

"And all the people said!" Irving Greene announced over the intercom.

"Amen!" The thousands cried out.

"Come on now, it's not a concert! Amen!" Greene tried to laugh and encourage the crowds to cry out.

"Amen!" The cry was louder, but not inspired.

Greene was beginning to sweat wondering what might be happening around him.

"Let us sing tonight a song of our Church, of our

Foundation!" Greene pleaded more than asked. He started singing, but the music was hollow and the singing haunted. When it was finished, Greene hurried to his seat forgetting to introduce Joshua.

"Many here tonight." Joshua did not miss a beat and stood before everyone. "Have come worried about the Foundation concerning this man, Warren. You think you have lost confidence in the Foundation and I say we are as strong as ever. The man you fear is not here. This is the time of anti-Christ of Revelation. This is the time when the beast will show himself as the King of Kings only to deceive you to think that he is God himself. Don't trust that man or you will certainly perish."

The murmuring began to spread throughout the gathering.

"We are gathered here for a great work and a heavy task." Joshua raised his hands. "I have been authorized through fasting and prayer to lead you the way before judgement. It is up to us to take the anti-Christ out of our community of faith. We don't need such an abomination to toy with our faith so we rend ourselves apart. This hapless jester is dangerous only if you follow his objective to tear the Foundation asunder. He uses scripture to signify his own holiness."

More murmuring interrupted his words.

"I do not wish to play games any more with this man." Joshua lowered his hands and pointed to all of them. "This is insanity that is creeping into the helpless and ignorant."

There were a few 'Amens' and one or two soft 'Hallelujahs'. It appeared to Joshua that he was bringing them back to the Foundation.

"Those who are easily swayed into confusion do not know that eternity is at stake." Joshua became bolder in his words. "That man you call Warren cannot give you the security you need in this life. He is detrimental to the health and welfare of the Foundation and the World Church. The facts are strongly in favor of his guilt and his rhetoric point to his being an anti-Christ."

Behind Joshua, Grace stands to his right. Guards were surprised to see her wondering how she got on stage.

"No, no, no!" Joshua waved them all away. "Let her come forward."

Grace continued to stand her ground. John was there, also, yet kept his distance.

"Who are you?" Joshua addressed her though he felt uncomfortable looking behind her for others who might have broken the security field.

"Grace." She wasn't near the mike, but everyone heard her.

Everyone started to talk to each other now knowing who she was.

"You are Warren's friend?" Joshua thought fast how he could use her.

"Yes." Grace took a step closer.

"This is the friend of Warren who faked her so-called resurrection." Joshua turned to his audience. "I, your chosen of God tell you she is a fraud, too. Your way to paradise will not come through her."

"Nor you." Grace's voice eerily echoed off the buildings.

Some of the crowd almost cheered Grace on. Joshua could not let this event get out of hand.

"Take her away." Joshua called upon security.

"Stop! Release me!" Grace broke free. "Your time has come. Enjoy it while you can."

A sense of fear and agitation enveloped the crowds as they saw that Grace defied Joshua's authority and won. Grace raced offstage with John in tow. Security followed after them and soon had four officers joining in the chase.

"She's as mad as her leader." Joshua tried to quell the chaos that was beginning around him. "Do not turn your backs on me. Remember judgement will be the result if you insist on believing what you heard from her."

Already, some fights broke out.

"Please, I guarantee you peace!" Joshua started to panic. "Be not afraid! Do not go to the anti-Christ for your very souls are at stake."

The crowd started to calm down and look to Joshua for an explanation.

"Through me God speaks!" Joshua was almost desperate. "Listen to me! Look how he confuses and divides us. Stay with me and you will be rewarded."

••

John and Linda ran from the police to a concert where a choir and orchestra is playing Beethoven's ninth. It's a free concert sanctioned by the state. They run in and take the only two seats in the middle section between two other couples. As soon as they sit down they see the place surrounded.

"What are we going to do?" John is nervous and asks Grace since he was sure they were trapped. Lady on Linda's right shushes her.

John shakes his head and rubs his eyes. The last of the symphony is being played and the choir is magnificent.

"What shall we do, sir?" an officer asked Chief Andrews who took over the chase.

"Can you see them?" Andrews asked.

"No, sir." The officer saw little in the darkness.

"We'll have to wait then." Andrews was just as impatient.

"May I suggest we encourage them to sing the Hallejuah chorus?" He suggested.

"It's not sanctioned!" Chief exclaimed.

"We need these people." The officer stared at him

hard.

"What do you think will happen?" Chief asked.

"I think they will stand because they are cornered to make a statement." The officer explained.

"Make it happen." Chief nodded.

A pause at the end of Beethoven's Ninth. The audience applauded. The choir director was stunned as he was told by the officer to sing a banned piece of music. The choir director nodded and prepared the choir and orchestra. Then stood before the audience and said "We have a welcome addition to our concert tonight. The state has authorized us to sing a part of Handel's Messiah."

The audience gasped, but no one left. The music started. As Grace looked at John.

"What do we do? We're trapped!" John whispered loudly.

"We can't leave so let's go out in glory and acknowledge our Lord." Grace took his hand and prepared to stand as the first "Hallelujah" rang through the auditorium. Both the ma n on John's left and the woman on Linda's right grabbed their arms to keep them from standing. Four people in front of them stood up, then six others, then ten others until everyone was standing. John and Linda were allowed to stand last.

"This didn't go as planned." Andrews was upset.

"They'll run," assistant insisted.
"Watch closely then." Andrews ordered.

 "We have to go." John was anxious.

As they started the chief saw them and waved the officers to follow. As the first of the officers ran down the aisle some of the audience entered the aisle and lifted their arms obscuring the view of John and Grace. Soon the whole audience filled the aisles as John and Grace ran toward the exit.

"They're coming…" John cried out unsure they could escape.

"Keep moving." Grace noticed a difference in the people around them. Their faces seemed to shine in the dark. They made a path that led to the far exit as the group stood in the way of the police. They were able to escape into the night.

Don't let them get away!" Andrews tried to push his

way through the crowd. John and Grace did escape as they heard what sounded like trumpets. The police pushed their way through the crowd to the outside. They found no one in the streets and as Andrews cursed. he pulled the officers back inside to vent his rage at those inside. As he stormed into the auditorium he found no one there. No orchestra, no choir, no audience. Another trumpet sound was heard before complete silence.

Where do they go?" the chief was stunned.

"How could they leave so quickly?" the assistant was just as anxious.

"Call headquarters and find out what's going on?" Andrews looked around the auditorium seeing broken chairs, splintered stage and cobwebs, he wondered what had happened.

"They say thousands of people have disappeared from the city, sir." His officer had a confused look on his face.

"What are you talking about?" Andrews tried to call his office.

"I don't know." The officer shrugged.

"Let's go back and find out." Andrews stepped out into the streets as cars crashed into buildings and narrowly missed some of his men.

"This is insane!" They looked around in wonder as chaos overwhelmed the city.

Made in the USA
Charleston, SC
20 August 2016